SO-AAE-578

GREAT WALKS OF NORTH AMERICA

THE PACIFIC NORTHWEST

John McKinney

An Owl Book
Henry Holt and Company   New York

Henry Holt and Company, Inc.
Publishers since 1866
115 West 18th Street
New York, New York 10011

Henry Holt ® is a registered trademark
of Henry Holt and Company, Inc.

Published in Canada by Fitzhenry & Whiteside Ltd.,
195 Allstate Parkway, Markham, Ontario L3R 4T8

Library of Congress Cataloging-in-Publication Data
McKinney, John
Great Walks of North America: The Pacific Northwest/John McKinney.
1st ed.
p. cm.
"An Owl book."
Includes index
ISBN 0-8050-4420-5 (alk, paper)
1. Hiking–Northwest, Pacific–Guidebooks.
2. Trails–Northwest. Pacific–Guidebooks.
3. Northwest, Pacific–Guidebooks.
I. Title.
GV199.42.N89M37 1997
917.95–dc21
97-2645

ISBN 0-8050-4420-5

Henry Holt Books are available for special promotions and premiums.
For details contact: Director, Special Markets.

First Edition – 1997

Designed by Kim Gendreau
Maps designed by Helene Webb

Printed in the United States of America
All first editions are printed on acid-free paper.

1 3 5 7 9 10 8 6 4 2

PHOTO CREDITS

Karin Dominello: 28, 42; Les Joslin: 64; Oregon Tourism Commission: 54, 77, 85; Portland, Oregon, Visitors Association: 100, 110; Seattle-King County News Bureau, James Bell: 132, 137; U.S. Army Corps of Engineers, Bill Johnson: 88; Washington State Tourism: 172, 177, 182. All other photos by the author.

"The serenity of the climate, the innumerable pleasing landscapes, and the abundant fertility that unassisted nature puts forth . . . render it the most lovely country that can be imagined."

—Captain George Vancouver
1792

ACKNOWLEDGMENTS

For their cooperation, field- and fact-checking and for generously sharing maps and interpretive information, the author wishes to thank the rangers and administrators of Oregon's state parks, the Portland Parks and Recreation Department, Crater Lake National Park, Olympic National Park, Mount St. Helens National Volcanic Monument, Mt. Rainier National Park, North Cascades National Park, Stanley Park, Pacific Rim National Park, and Garibaldi Provincial Park. A special tip of the hiker's cap goes to Monica Campbell-Hoppe and the Canadian Consulate General's Tourism Division, Manfred Schollerman and Rockwood Adventures of Vancouver, Glenn Milbury of Coastal Connections on Vancouver Island, the Seattle-King County Visitors Bureau, and the Portland, Oregon, Visitors Association. Pacific Northwesterners Gordon Black, Francie Petracca, Bob McDermott, Les Joslin, and Alice Mendoza added sunshine to my many walks in the rain. A final thanks goes to editors David Sobel, Jonathan Landreth and Cheri Rae for their deft editorial hands.

CONTENTS

OREGON

WASHINGTON

BRITISH COLUMBIA

INTRODUCTION

Mountains rise dramatically from the edges of the metropolae: The Coast Range thrusts skyward right behind Vancouver, Mt. Rainier and the Olympic Range loom tantalizingly close to Seattle, and on clear days, Mt. Hood and its snowy Cascade cousins seem to be only a stone's throw from Portland. Even when these mountains are enshrouded with fog, mist, and rain (as they often are), they still exert an intangible psychological, even spiritual force on residents and visitors alike.

All the jokes (and truths) about the region's considerable rainfall aside, the Pacific Northwest entices walkers with some of the world's most compelling terrain. This land of brooding skies, breathtaking coastlines and beckoning mountains offers strolls, saunters and hikes to remember.

"Would you like a relocation package?"

Seems like every time I popped into a local Chamber of Commerce/Visitor Center, cheerful assistants asked me if I wanted to relocate to their charming town. From Seaside to Sisters to Seattle, and from Bend to Bainbridge to Bellingham, the word is getting out that the Pacific Northwest is a great place to stay for a week—or even a lifetime.

Given the desirability of the Pacific Northwest lifestyle and its increasing popularity among those in the mood for moving, perhaps I shouldn't have been so surprised when I was offered as much information about homesites to see as sights to see. Certainly I noticed the steady stream of out-of-state cars pulling U-Haul trailers up the Oregon Coast Highway and along Interstate Highways 5, 84 and 90—presumably bound for the better life in the Pacific Northwest. And in many tourist publications, descriptions of each town's attractions and accommodations are followed by lists of Relocation Specialists, as realtors are known hereabouts.

In 1845, the prophetic Lansford W. Hastings envisioned current Pacific Northwest residents when he wrote in his *Emigrants Guide to Oregon*: "For so limited a population, there is a very fair proportion of talent and learning. And I may add, that the Oregon emigrants are, as a general thing, of a superior order to those of our people, who usually emigrate to our frontier countries. They are not the indolent, dissolute, ignorant and vicious, but they are generally enterprising, orderly, intelligent and virtuous."

A recent *Newsweek* magazine cover read: "Is everyone moving to Seattle?"

Not everyone. The headline might have been more accurate if it had asked: "Is everyone moving to the Pacific Northwest?" Actually, Vancouver is North America's fastest growing city.

The Pacific Northwest's three major cities are terrific places to walk and also superb bases for exploring the surrounding mountains and coast. Both Seattle and Vancouver boast dramatic waterside settings on their respective sounds, hilly suburbs high above the water, mountains and ocean, hiking and sailing oh-so-close to city center. Portland, situated on the riverfront, not the oceanfront, is probably America's most environmentally aware city. In the late 1960s, its ecologically enlightened citizens voted to tear down a freeway to create a riverside park.

The always civil (Pacific Northwesterners are known for their civility; perhaps they're influenced by the Canadians, among the planet's most polite people) visitor bureau employees were always just a little bit disappointed when I confessed I came to saunter not to settle, but quickly recovered and usually added something like: "Well, the Pacific Northwest is a wonderful place to walk, too. After you've hiked around maybe you'll find the grass is greener in _____."

Green is a key word to understanding the Pacific Northwest. While it's common enough for the new settlers to report they were drawn by the Pacific Northwest's economic opportunities (whether it's to become the next cyberspace entrepreneur or post-Grunge rock star), it's equally common to hear recent arrivals say they were lured by the mountains and the lush green environment.

In the rustic lobby of Lake Quinault Lodge, located in the Olympic rain forest, I spotted a young man, clad in checked shirt, jeans and hiking boots who was typing on a laptop computer. The scene would have been incongruous in other parts of America, but not in most parts of the Pacific Northwest where working in the woods has taken on a whole new meaning. Pacific Northwesterners are at once the most high-tech and the most outdoorsy in the nation.

"We just came up here to hike and hang out in the rain forest," Bret said sheepishly, closing his file, then his computer, as he spotted his wife, dressed for dinner, crossing the lobby. "But I have this report to finish. I'll modem it before we hit the trail." He gestured to the rain pitter-pattering outside the window. "Anyway, maybe tomorrow won't be such a bad day to work. It's supposed to rain all weekend."

While increasing numbers of workers now log-on to begin their day, a substantial number would rather simply log. The computer has not yet completely supplanted the chain-saw as a symbol of Northwest industry. What that means, of course, is that not all is beautiful in the Pacific Northwest. Seattle's Microsoft Corporation, personification of the Information Age economy, is located but 55 miles as the eagle flies from the logging town of Forks. While three million people around Puget Sound have advanced from an agricultural economy to a manufacturing economy to a service economy and now on to an Information Age economy, the people in the Olympic timber towns are stuck three economies back, still cutting down trees in third world fashion and shipping them overseas.

No wonder, as a ranger told me at the Hoh Rain Forest Visitor Center, visitors often seem surprised to find a forest intact. Just outside Olympic National Park lies a part of Washington that breaks the heart. Dodging logging trucks on Highway 101, motorists observe textbook examples of deforestation. Here is roadside indictment of twentieth-century forestry practices: clearcuts (Past Forestry), checkerboard clearcuts (Present Forestry), and industrial tree farms (Future Forestry), where young crops of Douglas fir are planted in straight rows like corn.

Fortunately the Barons of Logland have been increasingly out-legislated, out-lawyered and out-lobbied by conservationists in recent years. The standing of the region's trees has been increased by court decisions and in the eyes of visitor bureaus who now understand that while ancient forests can be sold to mills only once, they can be sold to millions of visitors over and over again.

Many would-be visitors figure that all the Pacific Northwest offers, as a walking destination anyway, is a wilderness of trees, trees and more trees. Certainly the region boasts forests galore, including North America's only rain forest. But the scenery is by no means limited to tall timber. Volcanoes, wilderness beaches, roaring rivers, alpine meadows, deep lakes and some of the greenest cities in North America are attractions for walkers. An obsessive hiker could spend an entire summer just visiting glaciers or hiking to hot springs. "Collecting" waterfalls is wonderful sport in the Pacific Northwest. The waterfall walker could begin with some of the big names—Latourell and Multnomah Falls in the Columbia Gorge, Comet Falls in Mt. Rainier National Park, and Rainbow Falls in North Cascades National Park—then hike to a hundred more.

Regional appellations such as the "American Southwest" or "New England" are far from exact terms, but they are more specific than "Pacific Northwest" which can be defined a half-dozen ways or more depending on one's geographical biases. All agree that Oregon and Washington are at the core of the Pacific Northwest. Some include Montana, Idaho, British Columbia and the Yukon. Some extend the Pacific Northwest as far northeast as the Canadian Rockies, as far northwest as Alaska, as far south as northern California. I would call such expanded versions the "Great Northwest," but not the Pacific Northwest, which more properly includes the coast, the Coast Range and the wet, western side of the Cascades.

My version of the Pacific Northwest, as covered in this book, is relatively conservative. Vancouver Island marks the northern boundary, Oregon's border with California forms the southern boundary. The western boundary is, of course, the Pacific and the eastern boundary is the crest of the Cascade Range. Much of what I define as the Pacific Northwest is called "Ecotopia" by author Joel Garreau in his landmark book, *Nine Nations of North America*. Even so limited, the Pacific Northwest includes lots of room to roam, a lush, 600-mile long corridor between Pacific breakers and Cascade peaks.

Until Alaska became a state, the Olympic Peninsula was the wild northwest corner of the United States; in many respects, it still is. Washington's wilderness coast delivers not only continental America's westernmost point (at Cape Alava) but its northernmost point at Cape Flattery.

The varied elevations and landscapes of the Pacific Northwest comprise several walking seasons. The shortest is that of the high Cascades peaks, ten weeks of flower-filled meadows from mid-July through September. At lower elevations, such locales as the Olympic Rain Forest and the Rogue River may be accessible for six months or more, from about May through October. Year-round hiking in and near cities—Portland, Seattle, Victoria and Vancouver—is possible all year with the right rain gear. The Oregon and Washington coasts are accessible all year around, too, but can be mighty rainy.

The Pacific Northwest boasts many of the nation's superlatives: Most glaciers (North Cascades National Park); the only rain forest in North America (Olympic Peninsula); the most environmentally oriented outdoor sculpture (Portland) and the most recent volcanic eruption (Mount St. Helens).

Some great walks of the Pacific Northwest have marquee value around the world: the Wonderland Trail around Mt. Rainier, the West Coast Trail on Vancouver Island, and the Mount St. Helens' summit climb. Along with the world's tallest Douglas fir (Olympic National Park) and America's deepest lake (Crater), the Pacific Northwest offers lots of room to roam. The state of

Oregon and the country of Germany are about the same size, but Germany's population is more than 20 times larger. Vancouver Island, North America's largest island by far, is bigger than Holland.

Vast tracts of officially designated wilderness are unsullied by twentieth-century developments, yet are accessible to visitors by virtue of good roads and a fine system of state and provincial parks, national forests and national parks. These parks, preserves and special places provide enough great walking to last a lifetime.

Great Walks offer challenges—and rewards.

About the series

Inspiration for Great Walks of North America came on a walk, of course. While trekking through the wet and wild Virgin Narrows in Zion National Park, I fell in step and into conversation with a group of German and English hikers, who told me they journeyed to America to explore some of the country's best pathways. These enthusiastic Europeans raved about America's superb trail system, but complained that the available trails information, sometimes voluminous, sometimes scanty, did not highlight the very best hikes in the region.

Finding the best walks in trails-rich regions such as the Southwest, the Pacific Northwest or New England is a daunting task. No other country has a trails system with the diversity that's found in the U.S. These paths, some celebrated, some obscure, explore the most stunning landscapes in America.

The books in the Great Walks series are designed to provide detailed introductions to America's major trails and best walks, as well as to explore this country's regions in all their diversity. Later volumes will embark on great walks around the world.

For those who love to walk, but don't know where to go, each guide is a primer for beginners, a ready reference for the experienced, a book of dreams for the armchair traveler. Drawing upon my miles of lengthy personal experience, travels, and years of research, the books provide trail-specific data on mileage and elevation gain, season, terrain, plants and wildlife, historic and scenic highlights.

In 1986 I began sharing my adventures afoot with *Los Angeles Times* readers in a weekly hiking column. For the first few years, these adventures were strictly local—walks around Southern California. The column was, is, extremely popular. Local parks often assigned extra rangers on weekends when my hiking column sent readers to their neck of the woods.

It wasn't long before I created a new dilemma: My readers it seems, like walkers everywhere, are a rather sophisticated, mobile lot, who like to get out of town—far out of town in many cases, and take hiking holidays and walking tours all over the West, the nation, the world.

And so I began to walk about and write about New England and New Zealand, North Sea islands and South Pacific islands, the Everglades and the Olympic rain forest. Again, the response was overwhelming. Visitors bureaus, tourism offices, national parks and walking tour companies were flooded with calls from curious walkers after one of my newspaper columns described a particular destination.

During my talks to hiking clubs and nature groups, and as a guest on radio and TV interview programs, I was often asked about my favorite walk in New England, the Rockies, British Columbia or Hawaii. Response to articles I wrote about walking in far-flung destinations for national magazines offered further convincing testimony about American walkers' willingness to travel to a different part of the country, even a different continent to take a great walk.

Once, before railroad tracks, roads and runways began whisking us to our destinations at landscape-blurring speeds, footpaths linked people and places across the land. These trails—some well-known routes, others nameless pathways—were often difficult for early pioneers, but they gave users an intimacy with the land and a social interaction with others that we moderns can only imagine.

Now, millions of Americans, joined by visitors from other lands, are rediscovering America's national history and natural history by walking these storied paths. Now, the adventurous walk by choice, not out of necessity. Going there, rather than getting there, is the goal.

Americans began walking for recreation in great numbers in the early years of the twentieth century. In 1910 the Green Mountain Club of Vermont blazed the first extensive nature path, from the Massachusetts to the Canadian borders. A few years later the Appalachian Trail was built and Americans from shore to shore began hiking for recreation—a phenomena that has grown exponentially every decade since.

In 1968, the U.S. Congress approved legislation creating the National Scenic Trails System and placed the Appalachian Trail and the Pacific Crest Trail under the stewardship of the U.S. Department of the Interior. Congress also authorized a system of shorter footpaths called National Recreation Trails. To date, America has eight National Scenic Trails and more than 700 National Recreation Trails.

Each year brings the heartwarming story of someone who walks for an entire summer or for six months, for a thousand or two thousand miles on one of America's long-distance trails. Most walkers, however, are not "end-to-enders," but day hikers, weekenders or week-long excursionists. These enthusiastic, but often pressed-for-time walkers want to know the very best walks in the most beautiful places.

Each book in the Great Walks series is a natural history road map to memorable landscapes, highlighting singular examples of geology, flora, fauna and scenery.

Read them for inspiration before you set off, for reference while on the trail, or as armchair travel between getaways. The Great Walks books are a walker's best guide when planning a short getaway or long vacation. Sit back and relax, and when you've read enough, take a hike through America's most beautiful landscapes.

Great Walks

What is a great walk?

It's a question as difficult to answer, as unanswerable perhaps, as "What is great art?" or "What is great music?" Objectivity in these matters is impossible, statistical analysis inappropriate, a rating system downright ridiculous.

Some insight into what comprises a great walk comes from my range of field experience. I've explored considerably more than a thousand trails in America, plus many pathways abroad during a 20-year span as a "walking writer." Most, if not all, of these trails had one or more distinctly pleasurable sights and at the very least offered some good exercise.

I've also discussed the notion of a great walk at some length with dozens of trail builders, fitness consultants, park service professionals, and experienced hikers. No two experts agreed what defined a great walk, of course, but some common themes emerged.

Elements contributing to a great walk are:
- Unusual landforms
- Forests, ancient or at least mature
- Wildflowers
- Intriguing flora
- Splendid views
- Lakes, rivers, ocean shores
- Tranquillity and solitude
- Wildlife watching
- Cultural or historical interest

To help pick the best walks in a region, I relied heavily on the advice of National Park Service rangers, Forest Service naturalists, Sierra Club outings group leaders, nature center directors, professional tour leaders, and many local hikers. Nevertheless, final selection of this book's walks was mine and the many outdoors consultants who aided me should be thanked for their invaluable expertise and be held blameless for my admittedly subjective decision-making process.(Perhaps my most difficult task was limiting the number of walks in the splendid region described in this book.)

Quite apart from our not-very-scientific criteria, a great walk often depends on what a walker brings on the walk. No, I'm not referring to a hiker's knapsack packed with lunch, water bottle and compass, but to the point-of-view a walker brings to the great outdoors. Some walkers are looking for romance, some for trout, some for leg-stretchers to break up a vacation drive, some for a week-long hike that's a vacation from driving.

A great walk for a family might be one in which baby can come along, perched happily in a backpack; or one that tires out a four-year old so he'll nap in the car during the two-hour drive back to the motel; or a stirring sojourn that puts a smile on the face of even the most sullen teenager.

The Great Walks guides are designed to offer a diversity of walks: easy family jaunts along the coasts and in national parks, middle-distance day hikes with multiple options, challenging day hikes, and even some multi-day backpacking treks.

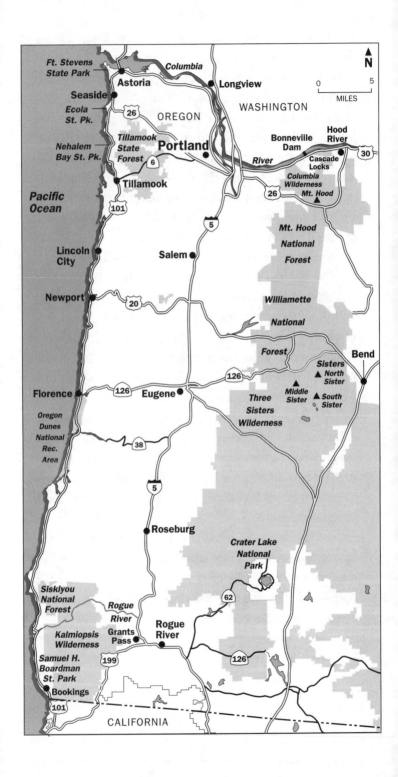

OREGON

Majestic bluffs overlook Oregon's rugged coastline

OREGON COAST

CHAPTER ONE

OREGON COAST

Like so many travelers, I'd driven Highway 101, the Oregon Coast Highway, which puts most of the beach within reach, and taken a few hurried day hikes. But I wanted the best of the West Coast, so I turned to Oregon Coast Trail expert Pete Bond.

"Walking the trail is a chance to experience the Oregon Coast in all its diversity," explains Bond, Ocean and Recreational Trails coordinator for the state parks system. "Hikers can walk grassy headlands, around bays and estuaries, through old-growth fir forests, and along empty beaches."

The Oregon Coast Trail laces together resorts and historic fishing villages clustered around the mouths of rivers feeding into the Pacific, miles of sandy beaches, cobbled shore and bold headlands. The names along the trail are almost irresistible to a coast walker: North Spit, Yachats, Yaquina Head, Devil's Punchbowl, Dragons Teeth, House Rock and Hug Point.

The Oregon Coast Trail logo bears a distinct resemblance to a 1960s peace symbol, as if the trailblazers and park bureaucrats who launched the path in the 1980s were veterans of the anti-war movement. Onetime peace advocates now promoting trails?

The walking is much easier now than in 1806 when Captain William Clark wrote: "Sea looked wild breaking with great force against the scattering rocks and the rugged rocky points under which we were obliged to pass and if we had unfortunately made one false step we should inevitably have fallen into the sea and dashed against the rocks in an instant . . ."

The most exciting and longest uninterrupted stretch of the 350-mile long trail, explains Bond, is the well-signed, 60-mile long coast path extending from Tillamook Bay to the Columbia River at the Washington border

After a couple of drives up and down the Oregon Coast Highway, and a lot of day hikes along the way, Bond's recommendation of the far north coast as the best stretch to walk rings true. The south coast is pleasant enough, but crowded near the coast highway and, although proud Oregonians would bristle at the notion, very much an extension of Northern California. Oregon's central coast sometimes impresses me as being a little too...well, Oregonian, with its logging museums, logging trucks and the stench of paper mills. All manner of four-wheeled vehicles assault the famed Oregon Dunes and, while the majority of this majestic ecosystem is off-limits to off-roaders, the balance is one of the West Coast's most popular places for a spin on the sand. (I hate to see vehicles on the shore—perhaps a reflection of my having been raised in Los Angeles where the only place you *couldn't* drive was on the beach.)

Yes, it's the northern coast that offers the wildest walking. This coast proved a little too wild for continent-crossers Merriwether Lewis and William Clark whose expedition was too exhausted and rain-soaked to explore the west coast, once they reached it.

Lewis and Clark spent the miserable winter of 1806 at Fort Clatsop, located north of present-day Seaside. Driven mad by a constant diet of fish and by feet-rotting fungi, the explorers' diaries record only twelve days without rain. Of all the real estate the two explored for President Jefferson, this Oregon coast seemed the most ill-suited to settlement.

Most winters are milder than the one of 1806. Some winter weeks it doesn't rain, and daytime temperatures in the 50s F. are pleasant for the walker. The Oregon Coast Trail is open all year. Many hikers suggest autumn is the best season for a hike when the skies are clear and the beaches are empty.

Spring is a volatile time on the Oregon coast, a time between winter storms and summer fog. The wind howls off the Pacific, painting dramatic seascapes, the waves churning up the cold gray-blue ocean, whipping the water into froth and heaving the surf onto shore.

Sometimes before a storm, after a storm, or between storms, the coast is almost disturbingly tranquil and around the walker unfolds what the locals call a "Blue Hole." The wind eases, the sky clears, and the sun makes the wet rocks sparkle and the conifer forests lining coastal cliffs glisten. On such days, mountains loom up to the east, hovering over the coast and creating a scene reminiscent of Oahu.

Were it not for these storms, for a dark season that may last five months or more, Oregon's coast might resemble California's; Astoria might have become San Francisco, Tillamook Bay might be "the Big Sur of Oregon," and Cannon Beach "The Carmel of the Oregon Coast." But these storms are the very essence of the Oregon Coast, as much a part of the walking experience as the rocky shores, the sandy beaches and the splendid Oregon Coast Trail.

Samuel H. Boardman State Park

Oregon Coast Trail

To House Rock Viewpoint is 3 miles round trip; to Miner Creek is 7 miles one way.

This 11-mile stretch of Oregon Coast is a dramatic tableau of wooded cliffs, grassy headlands, steep canyons, small beaches and rock islands. Samuel H. Boardman, Oregon's first state parks superintendent, was so impressed with the beauty of this length of coast that he not only worked diligently to acquire the land for the public, but pressed the U.S. Department of the Interior to consider it for national parkland.

Boardman, who directed Oregon's parks from 1929 to 1950, failed to convince federal officials to embrace his cause; his fellow Oregonians, however, did establish a state park in his name.

The segment of Oregon Coast Trail (OCT) extending through the park is one of the best in the state. It's not your basic breezy beach walk; it dips in and out of steep canyons and visits a variety of terrain.

OCT crosses grassy blufftops on its 1.5-mile journey to House Rock Viewpoint. Beyond, the path passes through stands of spruce and grassy meadows. Hit the beach for another 1.5 miles, glimpse Whalehead Island, a Moby Dick-profiled offshore rocky and continue to the odd Indian Sands, pine-fringed sand dunes. Hike over more wind- and wave-sculpted headlands to the north trailhead at Miner Creek.

Access: Samuel H. Boardman State Park is located a few miles north of Brookings. Lone Ranch, a shoreline picnic area near Cape Ferrel, is the southern trailhead for the park's segment of OCT.

33

Oregon Dunes
National Recreation Area

Overlook Beach, Tahkenitch Dunes, Threemile Lake Trails

2 to 6.5 miles round trip.

Forty miles of sand dunes extending from Florence to North Bend attract hikers to Oregon Dunes National Recreation Area. Oregon's shoreline Sahara is a land of oblique dunes, marshlands and odd forested islands on the sand. This weird landscape is said to have prompted Frank Herbert to write the science fiction classic, *Dune*.

Most of Oregon's shore is too precipitous and too rocky to gather much sand, but here the combination of a flat coastal plain lodged between two rocky points and brisk winds, makes for lots of it. Some of the dunes measure more than four hundred feet high and a mile wide.

While you'd guess that the dunes would be a compelling vista for motorists traveling Oregon's coastal Highway 101, in fact very little of the national recreation area is visible from the road. Ecologists know that the dunes have engulfed--and are engulfing--giant conifer forests; from the motorist's view, however, it looks like the trees along the highway are marching across the dunes.

How to get to the dunes? An answer to this question, as well as any others can be found at the National Recreation Area Visitor Center in Reedsport.

In response to the where-are-the-dunes? question, the Forest Service established the Oregon Dunes Overlook. About halfway between Reedsport and Florence, a well-signed turnoff from Highway 101 leads to the overlook, which features four levels of platforms connected by wooden walkways. In the summer months, Forest Service interpreters give talks about the dunes.

Bird-watchers flock to the dunes to count the 250 species found near the recreation area's lakes, creeks, wetlands and shoreline. At the mouth of meandering creeks, bald eagles and egrets dive for fish. Migrating Canada geese rest and feed in the estuaries. Majestic tundra swans winter in the marshes along the Siuslaw River at the north end of the national recreation area.

Hikers, however, are more likely to hear the honking of motorists than the honking of geese. More than a third of the dune system is open to off-highway vehicles.

While zooming over the sand in noisy dune buggies and ATVs does not lack for enthusiasts, the best way to appreciate the dunes is on foot. Short footpaths lead

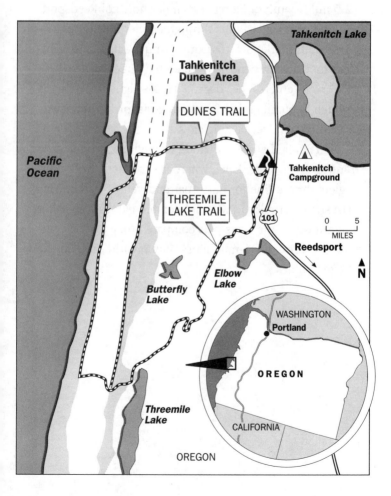

along creeks and through the forest to the great sand mounds, but no trails actually traverse the dunes. A pair of binoculars and a compass can help you stay oriented in the frequently fog-bound sandscape.

Overlook Beach Trail is one mile to the beach. You can see almost the entire trail from the upper deck of the Oregon Dunes Overlook, located on the west side of Highway 101, 10 miles south of Florence or 10 miles north of Reedsport. Some of the route across the dunes is marked with poles topped with blue bands.

Tahkenitch Dunes Trail is two miles to the beach. Find the signed trailhead parking area in the Tahkenitch Campground on the west side of Highway 101, some 12.5 miles south of Florence, 8 miles north of Reedsport.

The path leads a mile through conifer forest then follows route markers across quiet dunes (closed to vehicles) to a dogleg bend in Tahkenitch Creek near where the creek enters the ocean. Heed signs (March 15 through September 15) instructing visitors to stay away from snowy plover nesting sites.

Threemile Lake Trail winds through spruce forest to tranquil Threemile Lake where river otters frolic and anglers drop a line for cutthroat and yellow perch. This path shares a trailhead with Tahkenitch Dunes Trail. After a quarter-mile the trails part company; they can be combined to form a 6.5-mile loop—my favorite hike in the Oregon Dunes.

 Oswald West State Park

Oregon Coast Trail

From picnic ground to Neahkanie Mountain summit is 7.6 miles round trip.

Oswald West State Park was named for Governor Oswald West who, way back in 1913, proclaimed the Oregon beaches public property. Every state with an ocean beach should be so lucky.

Coastal trails meander through old growth forest of towering spruce. During a storm in 1982, with winds in excess of 150 mph, some of the giants were flattened; others, miraculously withstood the assault. From the edge of the wind-bowed but unbroken forest on Cape Falcon, hikers get terrific tree-framed coastal vistas. The 1.8-mile trail to the cape climbs through an ancient forest of western hemlock, cedar, and fir.

A good place to get the big picture of the northern Oregon coast is from Neahkahnie Mountain, "Home of the Gods," in native American legend. Viking-designed bronze tools were found at the base of the mountain, leading to speculation that Norsemen landed on these Oregon shores about 1010 A.D.

A rewarding segment of the Oregon Coast Trail travels to the storied mountain; the path passes through woods to Neahkahnie Punchbowl, a cliff-edge meadow, then to the highway, 1.3 miles from the trailhead. The well-engineered trail with some modest switchbacks takes you 2.5 miles to the top. From the 1,661-foot summit are glorious views of the Oregon Coast, south to Cape Meares 25 miles away.

Access: Oswald West State Park is located off US 101, some 10 miles South of Cannon Beach.

 Tillamook Head

Oregon Coast Trail

From Ecola Picnic Area to Tillamook Head is 5.6 miles round trip; to Clark's Point is 7.6 miles round trip; to north trail-head/Seaside is 6.9 miles one way.

Ecola State Park has an excellent trail that explores "the Big Sur of Oregon." The rugged Tillamook Head offers intermittent vistas toward Astoria and the mouth of the Columbia River.

Tillamook is a name familiar to travelers, or to cheese lovers anyway, because the Tillamook Creamery Association spends a lot of money on advertising. Tillamook County is dairy country, where cows outnumber people. "Trees, cheese, and ocean breeze" is the local Chamber of Commerce slogan.

Tillamook Head is a dramatic intrusion into this Wisconsin-by-the-sea. It's a huge hunk of basalt, a volcanic curiosity of the Coast Range; the head is positioned in such a way that it resists erosion by the relentless waves.

Tillamook Rock Lighthouse sits on a basalt island about a mile offshore. Built in 1879, Terrible Tilly withstood a number of storms that sent waves crashing over the top of her. She was retired in 1957, and promptly purchased by a group of Las Vegas businessmen--for what purpose no one seems to know. After a couple of ownership changes the still privately owned rock is now used as a columbarium, that is to say, a vault with niches for urns containing cremated ashes. The way waves crash against the base of the lighthouse, one imagines that this is not a particularly restful place to spend eternity.

The Oregon Coast Trail in the park is first a little-trafficked park access road along the beach, then a lovely trail through a lush rain forest of spruce and fir, salal and salmonberry. A 6.9-mile length of the path is designated a National Recreation Trail in honor of its stunning scenery. It's wild, wet and often muddy, even in summer, but not particularly strenuous.

The path traces about the same route over Tillamook Head taken by explorers Lewis and Clark in 1806. Encountering the native Tillamook people, the famed party bartered for a couple hundred pounds of blubber from a beached whale.

Ecola State Park took its name from the whale (ekoli in the Tillamook tongue), and the park is an excellent spot from which to observe migrating grays.

From the park picnic area, the blufftop path serves up some terrific ocean views as it travels to Indian Beach. Next, the coastal trail climbs to a trail camp atop Tillamook Head. Another mile of travel delivers the hiker to the 1,000-foot Clark's Point of View, and a vista William Clark pronounced "most pleasing" in his diary.

This is a good turnaround point for an out-and-back day hike. If you've made transportation arrangements, hike the final 3.1 miles of trail to the outskirts of Seaside. The path alternates between ancient forest and breathtaking open areas with superb views.

Access: From Highway 101, two miles north of Cannon Beach, turn west into Ecola State Park. To reach the northern trailhead, follow Sunset Boulevard south from Seaside to the signed parking area.

 Oregon Coast Trail

From Tillamook Bay to Columbia River is 60 miles one way.

The most exciting, and longest uninterrupted stretch of the 350-mile long Oregon Coast Trail opines Pete Bond, Oregon State Parks trails expert, is the well-signed, 60-mile coast path extending from Tillamook Bay to the Columbia River at the Washington border. Many a B&B has sprung up along this length of coast, which appeals to those hikers looking for a good meal, a hot shower and comfortable bed at the end of a long day of coastal hiking. The trail, plus the nearby amenities add up to a terrific European-style inn-to-inn adventure, Bond suggests.

"The trail gives walkers the chance to explore some wonderful small towns, sample the local cuisine and hospitality," declares Bond, who stresses the path is more a cultural experience than a wilderness trek.

The walker may begin with a trek around Tillamook Bay some fifteen miles on the shoulder of Highway 101 back through Tillamook to the town of Garibaldi. Alternatively, one may walk up the seven-mile long Tillamook sandspit to its end, then flag a passing boat for a ride to the Garibaldi Marina. Failing to attract a passing boat means returning the way you came; this will result in a fourteen-mile hike with absolutely no northward forward progress.

I felt lucky so I walked up the sandspit, first on a gated road, then over a sandy beach along Tillamook Bay. Two and half hours of walking brings one to the end of the sandspit. I flagged a ride, hope you do, too.

Walk into Garibaldi, named by the town's non-Italian founders after Giuseppi Garibaldi, who, it seems was a fisherman before he united Italy. Garibaldi has gone the way of many an Oregon settlement, a metamorphosis from lumber town to commercial and sportfishing center. No condos or vacation homes here, but mill workers'

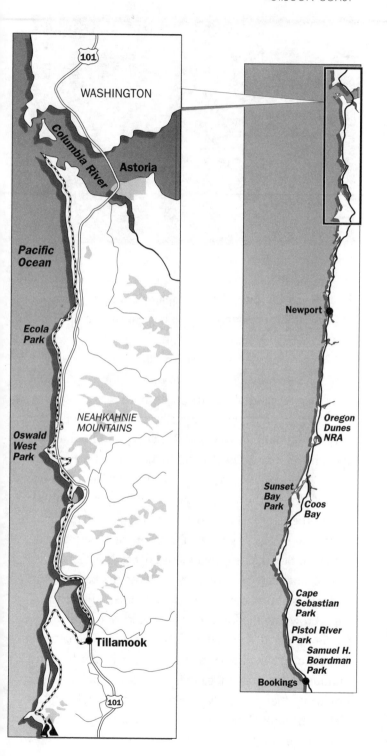

Unlucky boat near Cannon Beach

houses still line the bluffs—bargains I suppose for relo-
cating Californians who want to be near the sea but don't
want to live in a boutiqued resort.

From Garibaldi, you beach-walk north in an almost
straight line, walled off from the coast highway and most
signs of civilization by a string of sand dunes.

Nostalgic-for-New York-walkers will no doubt be
surprised to find the towns of Rockaway and Brighton on
the Oregon Coast. The two destinations aren't reached by
the A train to Rockaway or the D train to Brighton,
though, but by the Oregon Coast Trail. Stop in Rockaway
to call the Jetty Fishery Ferry to tell them you're hiking
their way. They'll give you a boat ride across long
Nehalem Bay, the drowned mouth of the Nehalem River.
As the small ferry transports you across the bay, look up
at some beautiful dairy cow country, emerald green pas-
tures crowding the four-foot high banks of the bay.

From this delightful dairyland, walk into Nehalem, a
hamlet of planked sidewalks fronting recently fixed-up
antique shops and art galleries. A good place to bunk
down is the spotlessly clean and amazingly cheap
Nehalem Bunk House, a rustic motel with an adjoining
espresso parlor.

Next morning, get buzzed by a triple latte and hike up the Nehalem Bay's sandspit into the wind. "Sandblast State Park" they ought to call it.

OCT passes the trail to Neahkanie Mountain, then stays in old growth forest in the company of towering spruce, continuing to Oswald West State Park, named for Governor Oswald West who, way back in 1913, proclaimed the Oregon beaches to be public property.

The trail leads over Arch Cape then over Arch Cape Creek on a foot suspension bridge, then over the Hug Point headlands—not named for its romance, but for the necessity of wagons to "hug" the coastal bluffs at low tide in order to round the point.

Cannon Beach presents quite a different profile than any other town I've encountered on the Oregon Coast. Even from a distance, it looks...planned. Like a resort town should look. The Carmel of the Pacific Northwest seems to be successful at attracting the upwardly mobile from Portland, Seattle and San Francisco, with galleries, bookstores and bistros, located well away from the highway in a no-neon zone. Accommodations are good, if pricey. Wander down to the shore and walk a half mile south down to Haystack Rock, the 235-foot reigning monarch of the beach.

Next morning, cross the bridge over Elk Creek and enter Ecola State Park. In the park, the OCT is at first a little-trafficked park access road along the beach, then a lovely trail through a lush rainforest of spruce and fir, salal and salmonberry.

Follow the OCT past an old World War II bunker to the edge of Tillamook Head and marvel at Tillamook Rock Lighthouse, which sits on a basalt island about a mile offshore. (See Tillamook Head Walk)

OCT continues to Seaside, oldest resort town in the Pacific Northwest. Eccentric Portland railroader and ship-building mogul Ben Holladay developed Seaside in the 1870s as a resort, complete with the grand hotel

Seaside House, French chef, gaming rooms, a zoo and racetrack. Holladay's ships were ordered to fire cannon shots each time vessels sailed past the town. The opulence is long gone.

Oregon's apostle of haute cuisine, the late James Beard, once held his famous cooking classes in Seaside. Where did he eat? Well, there are a couple of places with good unadulterated-by-cornstarch-clam chowder, fried oysters and shrimp salad. City officials have fixed up Broadway, encouraged more upscale restaurants and motels and have been promoting Seaside as a conference center, but they haven't entirely succeeded, admits a bookstore owner. It's far from the ugliest coastal strip, but for someone into the flow of the Oregon coast, and its rhythm of tides, Seaside is jarring.

Broadway's "Million Dollar Walk," is not so much garish in its off-season emptiness as it is forlorn, a half-mile strip of arcades, corn dog stands, candy shops with 59 varieties of saltwater taffy, Funland ("Family Fun Since '31"), miniature golf, and skee ball joints intermingling with more upscale eateries, bookstores and espresso bars.

Spend the night at Seaside and push on.

Next morning, walk along Seaside's boardwalk (the only one in the Pacific Northwest) toward the more stately resort town of Gearhart, surrounded by the oldest golf course in the Northwest built here in 1892. It's tough to make par at the Gearhart links: there's not a gentle lie anywhere, and sand dunes everywhere. Adjacent to the course are stately bleached white and gray beachhouses of similar 1890s vintage now owned by well-to-do Portland families.

Begin your last long day along a long shore, a half-mile wide strand of beach that stretches fifteen miles to the Columbia River. Sometimes the military mind is hard to figure, you might muse when you reach Fort Stevens, a military outpost that guarded the mouth of the Columbia River from the Civil War through World War

II. While the Confederacy never even hinted it coveted Oregon, the Union Army built a huge base here to prevent Confederate ships from sailing up the Columbia. And what to make of Japanese naval strategy? In 1942, a Japanese submarine surfaced offshore and lobbed 17 five-inch shells, scoring a direct hit on the wire cage behind the batters box at the fort's baseball diamond. Ft. Stevens was the only military post in the lower forty-eight to draw hostile fire during World War II.

Beyond Ft. Clatsop, once occupied by Lewis and Clark Expedition, the last four miles of Oregon Coast Trail are along rolling sand dunes topped with coarse grass. Walk toward trail's end, pausing to view the barnacled exoskeleton of the Peter Iredale, a four-masted British vessel that lies half-buried in the sand, a 1906 casualty of the tidal tantrums between the Columbia River and the Pacific Ocean.

These two great bodies of water still collide with great violence today, the sight made all the more awesome by the dark sky and the driving rain. Look down at walls of breakers where the river crashes into tempestuous seas, up at a spruce forest all but lost in the clouds, then turn toward Astoria.

Top: On the trail near Paradise Lodge

Bottom: Rogue River Ranch

ROGUE RIVER

 **Rogue River**

Rogue River National Recreation Trail

40 miles one way.

A river runs through it—and a trail does too.

The Rogue has long been known as one of the Pacific Northwest's most renowned rafting rivers. Now its shoreline is fast gaining fame as a world-class walking destination.

In nature, as in art and industry, awards aren't always perfect indicators of achievement. In the Rogue's case, however, the river is most deserving of its considerable accolades. The river was designated "Wild and Scenic"—one of the first in the nation to receive this status when Congress created the Wild Rivers System in 1968. In later years, the footpath received National Recreation Trail status for its breathtaking scenery and the sterling hiking adventure it offers.

Rogue River National Recreation Trail is becoming increasingly popular for another reason: it offers lodge-to-lodge hiking for those who want great hiking by day and a hot meal and comfortable accommodation at night. A series of rustic Rogue resorts, spaced conveniently along the lower half of the trail and not-so conveniently along the upper half of the trail, offer a Euro-style walking experience in an all-American setting.

The trail offers a pleasant backpacking trip, too. Many small trailcamps are located by the Rogue or near frisky creeks that flow into the river.

Wildcat Rapids, Blossom Bar, Devil's Staircase and the Coffeepot are among the wet and wild challenges faced by rafters and kayakers. Between thrills and spills there's plenty of fine floating through more quiet waters. *The River Wild*, the 1994 movie starring Meryl Streep, began filming on the Rogue River, but filmmakers and environmental groups clashed and the production moved to Montana.

The two means of transport—aquatic and terrestrial—offer two different perspectives of the upper Rogue. Whether you're floating down it at a couple knots an hour, or hiking alongside it at two to three miles an hour, the upper Rogue is a river that captures your heart.

Rogue River National Recreation Trail follows the river's north bank for 40 miles. The path is sometimes known as the Upper Rogue River Trail, in part to distinguish it from a lesser counterpart trail along the lower Rogue River.

The trail passes through oak woodland and some stands of stately Douglas fir and western hemlock. Contouring over bare canyon walls, the path offers dramatic views of the river and rafters below and of high canyon walls towering up to 1,500 feet above the trail.

For much of its length the path stays 80 to 100 feet above the river, with occasional canyon wall climbs to 300 feet and frequent dips to the river. It's slightly easier to hike down-river than up; there's an elevation loss of 400 feet in the 40 miles between Grave Creek (elevation 650 feet) and Foster Bar (elevation 250 feet).

Spring is a splendid time to head for southwest Oregon. Long before the snow melts from the paths and passes of the Cascade Range, Oregonians in the know head for the Rogue River Trail. Days are warm (65 to 75 degrees F.) and the path is brightened with such wildflowers as Siskiyou iris and wild azaleas.

In summer the canyon gets quite hot and, while the trail is uncrowded, the camps and lodges en route are packed with river-runners. Autumn, before the onset of Oregon's infamous rainy season, is a fine time to hike the river trail.

Despite the increasing allure of the Rogue River Trail to hikers, it's the river rat pack (rafters, anglers, kayakers)

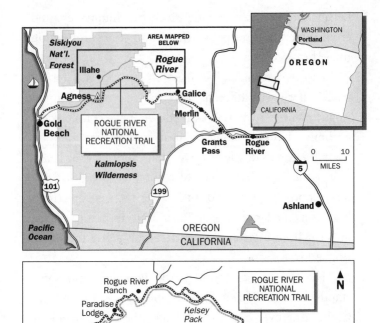

who run the show in terms of accommodations and logistics. This river traffic aids hikers, who can take advantage of the area's considerable number of commercial rafting outfitters and transport services. Huge meals served by the lodges are wolfed down with equal gusto by ravenous river-rafters and hungry hikers!

While logistics for a lodge-to-lodge hiking adventure can be complex, the hiker's mission is simple: Get transport as far up-river as you can walk down-river.

The Foster Bar (lower, western) trailhead is located some 30 miles up-river from the coastal town of Gold Beach. The Grave Creek (upper, eastern) trailhead is located 30 miles down-river from the city of Grants Pass.

Neither Grants Pass on Interstate 5 nor Gold Beach on Highway 101 will win your heart as a place to stay, but they are convenient jump-off places for a Rogue River adventure. If nothing else, Gold Beach excels at packing people onto jet boats and shipping them up-river.

The only other way to reach the river is via Marial Road which offers vehicle access to the Rogue's midsection. Within a short walk of the road meeting the river are the historic Rogue River Ranch, Tucker Flat Campground, Marial Lodge and Marial Forest Service Station.

In downstream order, the lodges are: Black Bar Lodge, Marial Lodge, Paradise Lodge, The Lodge at Half Moon Bar, Clay Hill Lodge Wild River Lodge, Illahe Lodge. Reservations are virtually mandatory for a stay at one of these lodges.

Hikers can enjoy Rogue River Trail in at least four different ways:

Weekend Lodge Trip (Two days, one night or three days, two nights). From Foster Bar, take the jetboat to Paradise Lodge. Spend the night. Day hike to Marial Lodge and Rogue River Ranch Museum (10 miles round trip), return to Paradise Lodge. Next day, hike 12 miles to Foster Bar. A night at the beginning or end of your trip at the Foster Bar-adjacent Illahe Lodge would be a pleasant way to ease into or out of the weekend.

Long Backpacking Trip (Four to five days, 40 miles one way). From Grave Creek, hike the whole length of Rogue River National Recreation Trail to Foster Bar. Numerous fine trail camps, some with developed water sources and bear-proof food storage facilities, are sited at convenient intervals. Camp cooking can be supplemented with meals and refreshments purchased from lodges located en route.

Weekend Backpacking Trip (Two days, 15 miles one way) Take advantage of the Marial Road entry to the riverfront and walk down-river to Foster Bar.

Long Lodge to Lodge Trip Alas, it's all but impossible for most lodge hikers to start at the Grave Creek Bridge Trailhead because it's a 24-mile hike to Marial, the first convenient lodge. (Black Bar Lodge is a perfect 9.6 miles

Friendly reception at Mule Creek Guard Station.

down the trail, but it's located on the opposite side of the river. If you can make some arrangements to get over to the other side and back, you can walk lodge to lodge along the whole river trail.)

Here's a capsule description of the trail: From Grave Creek, join Rogue River Trail west of the boat landing. The site is named after the grave of Martha Leland Crowley, daughter of a pioneer couple. A small trail camp is located a half-mile down the trail. The path's first five miles are quite rocky.

At mile 9.6 you'll see Black Bar Lodge opposite the trail on the south bank. The lodge is open from April through mid-November.

At mile 15.4 is Kelsey Creek Camp, replete with water supply. Mile 23.0, with the Rogue River Ranch Museum, is a hike highlight. Visit the old ranch and enjoy exhibits about Native American, river and ranch history. U.S. Bureau of Land Management caretakers voluntarily staff the Ranch.

At mile 23.4 is Tucker Flat Campground, a fine developed BLM facility, and at mile 24.3 is Marial Lodge. Just past the lodge is Mule Creek Guard Station, a Forest Service station staffed from June through September. The next couple of miles are particularly scenic as a cliff-edge trail travels above Mule Creek Canyon.

At mile 25.5 look for the Coffeepot, a churning whirlpool, and watch rafters bump and squeeze through the narrow passage. Mile 25.7 is breathtaking at Inspiration Point where the trail travels along a narrow ledge high on the cliff above the river. Blossom Bar Trail Camp, at mile 27.1, is a fine facility with water.

At mile 28.3, Paradise Bar, jet-powered mail boats bring passengers upstream to the handsome Paradise Lodge, the most hiker-friendly resort on the river. Campers will like the excellent camping at Brushy Bar, located along with a U.S. Forest Service station (staffed June through September) at mile 31.2.

At mile 33.2, find Clay Hill Lodge.

At mile 34.8, Flora Dell Creek, where a waterfall plunges over sheer wall into deep trailside pool. Beautiful!

At mile 39.0, a mile from trail's end, is Illahe Lodge.

Foster Bar, 40 miles out, has a developed campground.

Access: To reach Foster Bar from Gold Beach, turn east from Highway 101 onto Jerry's Flat Road (which eventually becomes Forest Road #33) and drive east 31 miles along the south side of the Rogue River. Cross the river on a bridge. Turn right and drive four more miles to the signed turnoff for the Foster Bar campground and boat launch. If you've made arrangements, the Paradise Lodge jetboat will pick you up at the small dock here for transport up-river.

To reach the beginning of Rogue River National Recreation Trail, walk back up the campground access road to the main road and follow it east, then north a half-mile to the signed trailhead.

New Pacific Crest Trail segment brings hikers closer to shore.

CRATER LAKE

CHAPTER THREE

CRATER LAKE NATIONAL PARK

If old Mt. Mazama had oozed instead of erupted, there would be no Crater Lake. But 7,700 years ago, the big mountain (Oregon's largest, some geologists believe) collapsed big-time, resulting in a caldera, then a lake and finally, a national park.

The cataclysm was a long time coming. Volcanic material had been building up Mt. Mazama for a half-million years before erupting with a volume estimated to be 50 times that of its more recently active Cascade cousin, Mount St. Helens.

After the hellacious firestorm, the volcano collapsed. The resultant six-mile wide caldera gathered rain and snowmelt and eventually filled to a depth of nearly 2,000 feet. Today Crater Lake is the deepest lake in America and the seventh-deepest lake in the world.

Because the huge, mesmerizingly blue oval has no inlets or outlets, and because not much vegetation grows along its shores, little organic material enters the lake. With little matter in suspension, the lake has a clarity that amazes. The rays of the sun can actually penetrate below the surface of the water and allow moss to grow at depths 450 feet in the clear lake.

Crater Lake's very depth (1,932 feet at its deepest point) is one reason why the lake is such a resplendent blue. Another reason has to do with the physics of light waves: longer light waves in the red, green and yellow part of the spectrum are more readily absorbed near the lake's surface than are the shorter blue-hued light waves which penetrate farther into the lake to excite the water molecules. Pick your blue adjective—azure, aquamarine,

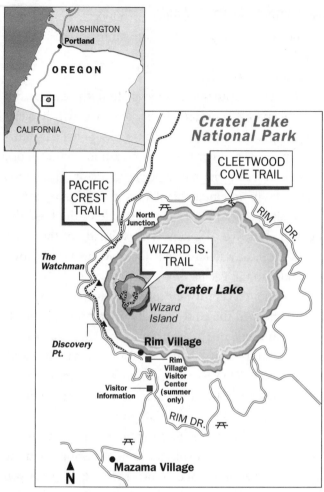

cobalt or cerulean—or simply conclude that Crater Lake has a blueness beyond words.

Crater Lake became the nation's sixth national park in 1902. It was one of the first parks "designed" by the National Park Service's newly created landscape architecture team. Just after World War I, team members toured European parks and art museums before setting to work at Crater Lake, where they designed Rim Drive and its scenic turnouts to make it easy for the visitor to get those postcard views.

By all accounts, the team did its job well. Maybe too well. Rim Drive makes lake views so easy to get that the average visitor spends only a few hours in the national park. Only a small percentage of modern visitors stay around to ask rangers, "What's there to see besides the lake?"

A lot, actually.

Few park visitors wander away from the caldera rim into the park's considerable backcountry which offers intriguing, and very likely solitary treks. Some adventurers explore the lunar-like, low-elevation (5,000 foot), Pumice Desert in the park's northern sector. The forests of Douglas fir, mountain hemlock and sugar pine, as well as the alpine meadows of the west side of the Cascades are also attractive to hikers. This wet side of the range births the headwaters of the Rogue River, which flows 150 miles to the Pacific.

For about a century, visitors and frustrated scientists have bemoaned the park's paucity of pathways. A handful of rim trails, one trail down to the lake and one on Wizard Island—that's about it for easy access to the park's main features. However, these rim trails are excellent, as are a number of nature trails and the summit climb to Mt. Scott, the park's 8,929-foot high point.

One of the park's most memorable walks is on Wizard Island, a small volcanic cone thrusting up in the western corner of the lake. In order to take this walk you must "endure" two more pleasures—a hike from the caldera rim down to the Cleetwood Cove boat landing and a fun boat tour of the lake that drops off hikers on Wizard Island.

For more than a half-century, the biggest disappointment to Pacific Crest Trail hikers was that the famed path (33 miles worth through the park) offered no views of the lake. In 1994, a new length of the PCT was built on the caldera rim and it delivers the long sought after lake views. As hikers discover it, this new beautiful and scenic stretch of PCT will likely become the park's premier footpath.

 Garfield Peak

Garfield Peak Trail

From Crater Lake Lodge to Garfield Peak is 3.4 miles round trip with 1,000-foot elevation gain.

Crater Lake views from the 8,054-foot summit of Garfield Peak can't be bettered. The islands—Wizard and Phantom Ship—and the whole caldera are at your feet. You'll also enjoy views of Rim Village and historic Crater Lake Lodge.

Northern vistas include two volcanoes—Mt. Bailey and Diamond Peak—while views to the south include the Klamath Basin and mighty Mt. Shasta.

Garfield Peak is the spot where photographers like to plant their tripods. While the popular Watchman and park high point Mt. Scott also offer good vistas, shutterbugs are forced to shoot into morning sun from Watchman, the afternoon sun from Mt. Scott; Garfield Peak, however, offers fine photo-ops all day long.

The peak's politic name arose in 1907 from a visit by Secretary of the Interior James R. Garfield. Whitebark pine, mountain hemlock and Shasta red fir cloak Garfield's slopes, while wind-stunted subalpine fir, scarcely bigger than bushes, are found near the summit. Spreading phlox, Applegate's paintbrush and many more wildflowers splash color along the trail.

The path, which begins behind the Crater Lake Lodge, maintains an assertive and constant grade. During summer months, rangers lead walks up Mt. Garfield.

Access: Park in Rim Village near the Crater Lake Lodge. The signed path begins on the east side of the lodge.

Mount Scott

Mount Scott Trail

From Rim Drive to Mt. Scott summit is 5 miles round trip with 1,200-foot elevation gain.

Park high point Mt. Scott is the summit to conquer not only for lake views, but also a panorama of surrounding summits and the entire national park backcountry. Clear-day views take in such distant Cascade peaks as South Sister, more than 80 miles north and Mt. Shasta, 100 miles south.

Geologists call Mt. Scott a satellite cone, fashioned by lava oozing laterally from Mazama's mammoth magma chamber. The cone was one of a cluster of volcanoes that once formed Mazama.

The trail to the 8,929-foot peak is a steady, steep (11 percent grade) climb past scattered whitebark pine. The last mile of switchbacks to the fire lookout will really get your heart pumping.

Before mid-July expect patches of snow. Unless you're an experienced mountaineer, avoid the mountain's north-facing snowfield.

Access: From Rim Village, drive 14 miles east on Rim Drive (0.2 mile past the Whitebark Pine Picnic Area) to a small turnout and signed trailhead on the right.

Cleetwood Cove, Wizard Island

Cleetwood, Wizard Island Trails

From Rim Drive to Cleetwood Cove is 2 miles round trip with 700-foot elevation loss; from Wizard Island Boat dock to summit is 2 miles round trip with 700-foot gain.

A jaunt to the lakeshore, a boat tour of the volcano and an island excursion add up to a day to remember.

Cleetwood Trail, even if it didn't lead to the tour boat dock, would be a popular trail because it's the only one that leads to the lake. Expect company. Some 500 people a day descend the mile-long trail to Cleetwood Cove. The walk is necessary to meet the tour boat so many a non-hiking tourist endures the trail.

While the path begins on one of the lowest routes on the caldera rim, it's nevertheless quite steep. The path drops down slopes forested in Shasta red fir and mountain hemlock, offering lake vistas from occasional openings in the forest. At trail's end are the boat dock and restrooms.

During the summer months, two-hour guided boat tours embark from Cleetwood Cove. The concessionaire-operated tours depart from 10 A.M. to 4 P.M., from early July to early September, weather permitting. Tour boats circle the water-filled caldera and stop at Wizard Island, where you can disembark. Remain on the island until the next tour boat—or the last tour boat of the day.

Wizard Island may have been named for its resemblance to a sorcerer's cap, but if you're a geologist you might figure that Cinder Island would be a more appropriate name. The isle is a true cinder cone; Crater Lake, in contrast, is actually a collapse-caused depression known as a caldera.

From the Wizard Island boat dock, the trail climbs for a few hundred yards then forks. The left fork leads a half-mile over lava blocks to Fumarole Bay, a popular, but extremely cold (55 degrees F. or less) spot to swim. The right fork switchbacks its way past scattered whitebark pine to the summit of the circular cinder cone. Crater Lake views from the island summit are memorable and unique.

Access: Follow Rim Drive 4.5 miles east from the north rim road junction to a large parking area.

Crater Rim, Discovery Point, Watchman Peak

Pacific Crest Trail

From Rim Village to Discovery Point is 2.6 miles round trip; to Watchman Lookout is 6 miles round trip; to North Junction is 12 miles round trip.

For more than a half-century, hiking the park's 33-mile length of Pacific Crest Trail was a so-so experience: water sources were scarce and the less-than-inspiring route was on fire roads. Worse yet, the trail didn't offer a single view of Crater Lake!

Crater Lake's Pacific Crest Trail—and hiker's perceptions of it—changed dramatically in 1994 when the National Park Service re-routed part of it to travel atop the caldera rim. A new length of trail was constructed from a trailhead off State Highway 62 to Rim Drive near Rim Village.

From the new south trailhead, PCT hikers can ascend to Rim Village. This path follows part of the same road to the rim that was built by U.S. Army troops in 1865.

If you can't spare the time for the whole new stretch of PCT or just can't wait to get those lake views, I recommend beginning your walk at Rim Village. The PCT leads through a forest of whitebark pine and mountain hemlock while serving up glorious panoramas of the water-filled caldera. Two must-see attractions on the lake rim are visited by the trail—Discovery Point and Watchman Peak.

Portions of the PCT route along the caldera rim utilize an old roadbed constructed by the U.S. Army Corps of Engineers in 1916; this road was the park's first "Rim Drive" until the present road was relocated farther away from the rim in the 1930s. At Discovery Point a plaque honors prospector John Hillman, first non-native to see Crater Lake in 1853.

PCT follows the rim to the shoulder of Watchman Peak. Join switchbacking Watchman Lookout Trail for the steep ascent to the summit. (Watchman is in the snow belt; sometimes snow keeps this trail closed until late July or until the park trail crew can clear a route to the top.)

The old fire lookout, built in 1932, offers great views of the lake and surrounding backcountry. Interpretive panels help to identify park landmarks.

Access: Begin from the trailhead at the west edge of Rim Village.

THREE SISTERS
WILDERNESS

CHAPTER FOUR

THREE SISTERS WILDERNESS

The Three Sisters Wilderness has long been recognized as something special by conservationists, its federal custodians, and even by Congress. A Primitive Area was established in 1937 and the area was one of the nation's first to receive protection under the landmark 1964 Wilderness Act. Expanded in 1977 and 1984, Three Sisters Wilderness now totals 286,708 acres, the largest such area in Oregon's Cascades.

Located in the Willamette and Deschutes national forests in central Oregon, Three Sisters is approached by two scenic roads—McKenzie Pass Highway (242) and Cascade Lakes Highway (46). Stop for trail information at the ranger stations in Sisters or Bend.

A handsome 40-mile stretch of Pacific Crest Trail crosses the wilderness, which is also blessed with 200 more miles of trail. Footpaths reach wildflower-strewn alpine meadows and inviting trail camps, give climbers access to challenging peaks and give fishermen access to 300 lakes.

Methodist missionaries named the trio of sisterly summits Faith, Hope, and Charity, but the names didn't stick. North Sister, the geologic elder, stands 10,094 feet, Middle Sister 10,053 feet. South Sister, at 10,358 feet, is both the highest and youngest of the three and presents the distinctly conical profile of your basic volcano. North Sister's summit has been severely eroded by glaciers and looks more like a volcano core than a volcano cone.

The volcanic trio is a treat for photographers, but a worry for scientists, some of whom fear the long-dormant Sisters might someday erupt like that suppos-edly extinct Cascade volcano, Mount St. Helens.

Certainly one of the most breathtaking views of the Sisters is from the town of the same name. Sisters (the town) also boasts vistas of Mt. Washington and Mt. Jefferson, Oregon's second-highest peak. The Sisters and surrounding summits, snowcapped for much of the year, form an awesome skyline for the little town.

The town, founded in the 1880s, served as a ranch-ing center and milltown before falling on hard times. It was rescued from boarded-up oblivion in the early 1970s and has since evolved into a resort village complete with art walks and music festivals.

Adding an exotic touch to this most American scene are the many llamas grazing in fields at the outskirts of town. Central Oregon—the Sisters area in particular—is the llama capital of North America.

Until the early 1970s, the South American creatures were considered zoo attractions, not working pack ani-mals. Sisters llama ranchers began breeding, raising and training the animals, creating a change in consciousness and a demand for more and more llamas. Now the sure-footed animals carry the cargo of families, fly fishermen, backpackers, and photographers. Public lands managers appreciate the llamas' low-impact on wilderness trails and herbage.

Les Joslin, retired U.S. Navy commander, got to know Three Sisters Wilderness very well some years back when at the Forest Service's behest he conducted a camp-site survey. Joslin's on-the-ground survey included hiking to all trailside lakes—and many lakes off the trail—in order to record and evaluate campground conditions and impacts to the ecology. Joslin walked a couple hundred miles, slapped at a couple thousand mosquitoes and emerged from the experience with both a thorough report and a heightened love for the land.

"If there's anything as satisfying as hiking in the

wilderness, it's working with people who appreciate the majesty of an environment like the Three Sisters," Joslin declares.

After Joslin's backcountry study, the Forest Service asked him to put his knowledge to good use in 1992 by staffing a new information station at the Three Sisters' major point-of-entry, the Green Lakes Trailhead. He and a group of volunteers are still at it. Concludes Joslin: "When hikers meet a helpful wilderness ranger, it adds to their experience and makes their trek all the more special."

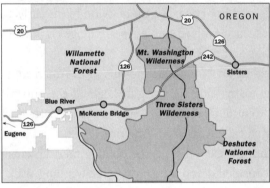

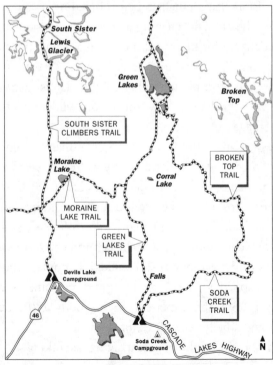

 Green Lakes

Fall Creek, Broken Top Soda Creek Trails
13-mile loop with 1,100-foot elevation gain.

Truly, they are green these Green Lakes, colored by ultra-fine silt ground by adjacent Lewis Glacier. Three Green Lakes, impounded by a 2,000-year-old lava flow, nestle in a glacier-scooped hollow between South Sister and Broken Top Mountain.

One of the wilderness area's most scenic trails climbs 4.2 miles to the lakes. The gorgeous route follows alongside a roaring creek, through a fir forest, and across a wall of obsidian blocks, the hardened lava that some 2,000 years ago flowed from South Sister.

Beauty you'll get from this trail, but not solitude. The route is the most heavily used in the Three Sisters WIlderness, where both day and overnight visitors are required to obtain self-issued wilderness permits at trailheads. Camping in the Green Lakes basin is restricted to designated campsites, and campfires are forbidden. Travel is restricted around some "restoration zones." September is the least-crowded summer month for backcountry exploration.

You can make this an 8.5-mile out-and-back day hike or follow a 13-mile looping return via Broken Top and Soda Creek trails. The looping return isn't quite as scenic, but you'll share the wilderness with fewer hikers.

The Green Lakes-bound path begins at Sparks Lake and ascends steeply alongside Fall Creek, a rambunctious watercourse of cascades and small falls. About two miles out, the path leaves the creek, passes a junction with Moraine Lake Trail, and heads around a glassy wall of black obsidian.

The main trail leads to the right (east) side of the lake. By linking a couple connector trails, you can loop around all three lakes while marveling at the mountain vistas.

When you're ready to leave Green Lakes, head east on Broken Top Trail for nearly three miles to a junction with Soda Creek Trail; follow this fairly easy pathway back to the trailhead.

Access: From Highway 97 in Bend, follow the well-marked 27-mile roadway to the Mt. Bachelor Ski Area. From here, drive 4.5 miles south on Highway 46 (Cascade Lakes Highway) to the signed Green Lakes Trailhead on the north (right) side of the highway. The large parking lot reflects this path's popularity. For a trail update, check in at the Wilderness Information station. Write your own day or overnight permit at the trailhead.

More than 300 lakes attract hikers to Three Sisters Wilderness.

South Sister Summit

From Cascade Lakes Highway to South Sister summit is 11 miles round trip with 4,900-foot elevation gain.

South Sister looks every inch a Cascade Range peak: a classic, sky-scraping volcano with a snowy cone and cinder-strewn slopes. Beautiful, and imposing. The 10,358-foot peak, Oregon's third highest, looks like it can be scaled only by technically skilled mountaineers.

Actually, South Sister is a walk-up. Not an easy walk-up, mind you, but an ascent within the abilities of the experienced hiker. Doggedness and desire will get you to the top.

Geologists say South Sister is the youngest of the Three Sisters; it's not been as glacially eroded as much as the other sisters, thus the volcano has kept its cone shape. South Sister's second claim-to-fame is that its summit crater rims Oregon's highest lake, Teardrop Pool. Reward for reaching the summit of South Sister is a majestic wilderness panorama.

From Devil's Lake Campground, it's a steep 1.3-mile walk up the South Sister Climber's Trail to a four-way junction with Moraine Lake Trail. The lake is a fine destination for a short (4 mile round trip) day hike.

Beyond the junction, the pathway to South Sister climbs ever more earnestly, reaching the 9,000-foot level as it approaches Lewis Glacier. The trail edges along the west side of the glacier before fading, then disappearing. Work your way up the cinder slopes and snow patches to the summit.

Access: From Highway 97 in Bend, follow the well-marked 27-mile roadway to the Mt. Bachelor Ski Area. From here, drive 6.5 miles on Highway 46 (Cascade Lakes Highway) to trailhead parking on the south side of the highway. Write your own day or overnight permit at the trailhead.

 Sunshine Meadows

Obsidian, Pacific Crest Trails

12 miles round trip with 1,200-foot elevation gain.

Climbers use Obsidian Trail to bring them near Middle Sister. Backpackers travel the trail to Sunshine Meadows in order to access paths leading to a multitude of wonders farther into the Three Sisters Wilderness. Day hikers revel in the trail itself, as well as the splendid alpine meadows.

If the array of trail users suggest a crowd, well, that's true. Entry into the area is by limited entry permit obtained in advance only at the McKenzie Ranger Station in McKenzie Bridge. Campfires are prohibited, and a camping setback of 100 feet from water and trails is enforced. Overnight visitors *passing through* the area, however, may enter with self-issued permits obtained at wilderness trailheads.

Ah, but the allure of Sunshine Meadows is considerable. From Sunshine, backpackers are tempted by several inviting locales reached by the famed Pacific Crest Trail. Head south five miles to Linton Meadows, between Middle Sister and The Husband. Northbound PCT traverses lava country to Collier Cone and vistas of Collier Glacier.

From Obsidian Trailhead, the popular pathway ascends 3 miles, crosses Jerry Lava Flow and then White Branch Creek. The trail forks after the creek crossing. Turn right on a continuation of Obsidian Trail, passing through a meadow. Obsidian Cliffs loom to the immediate west. The path travels 1.6 miles southwest to an intersection with the Pacific Crest Trail. Head left on the PCT, soon passing Obsidian Falls. After 1.5 miles on the PCT, just before Glacier Creek you'll reach a junction with Glacier Way Trail, a connector leading 0.6 mile back to reunite you with Obsidian Trail for your (probably reluctant) return to the trailhead.

Access: From McKenzie Highway (126) in the town of McKenzie Bridge, drive 5 miles east to a junction with Highway 242, which you follow 6 miles to the signed Obsidian Trailhead on the right side of the highway. Remember to call or stop in at the McKenzie Ranger Station, just east of McKenzie Bridge, for the required limited entry permit.

Tam McArthur Rim, Broken Hand

Tam McArthur Rim Trail
5.2 miles round trip with 1,200-foot elevation gain

Broken Top (elevation 9,175 feet) and its rocky appendage Broken Hand are in volcano country—a shattered world of red and black rocks. Broken Top's past eruptive behavior has peppered the area with "lava bombs," torpedo-shaped chunks of magma hurled from the volcano that cooled in flight. Years of erosion have exposed red and black cinders, as well as other evidence of this land's fiery history in the volcano's interior.

While in Sisters, the town, walkers quite naturally are desirous of getting a closer look at Sisters, the wilderness. This walk gets you closer. Tam McArthur Rim Trail is a grand ridgeline route that gives you close-up views of the buttes and craters of lava land, along with the Three Sisters and Mt. Washington.

After a 0.75-mile walk from the trailhead, the path leaves the lodgepole pine forest and climbs along the cliff edge of Tam McArthur Rim. Hikers leery of heights will stay back from the cliffs on the north side of the trail.

At the 2.5-mile mark, a quarter-mile connector trail leads north to a viewpoint. From here, you can retrace your steps back to the trailhead or, alternately, continue another mile along Tam McArthur Rim to the base of Broken Hand. Unless you're a rock-climber, this is the end of the hike. This last mile of Rim Trail is often snow-covered until the middle of summer.

Access: From downtown Sisters, follow Elm Street south, heeding signs directing you to Three Creek Lake. Drive 17 miles on Three Creek Road (otherwise known as Forest Road 16) to the signed trailhead and parking area. Write your own day or overnight permit at the trailhead.

MT. HOOD

MT. HOOD

What Mt. Rainier is to Seattle residents, Mt. Hood is to Portland: a dramatic landmark, a king of the Cascades, wilderness at the edge of the metropolis. Mt. Hood, Oregon's 11,235-foot high point nicknamed "the Fujiyama of America," beckons skiers, climbers and hikers to tour its middle and upper slopes.

Long ago Mt. Hood was an active volcano. Not-so-long ago (the mid-1800s) six minor eruptions were observed. When Mt. Hood's fumaroles began venting smoke in the 1980s, vulcanologists and seismologists rushed to install sensitive monitoring equipment to track the mountain's moods.

A major eruption would not endanger Portland's citizens per se, say planners with the Portland Office of Emergency Management. However, a Mt. Hood blast would wreak havoc with the city's water supply, Columbia River transportation and power generation, and devastate the logging and fruit-growing industries at the base of the mountain.

Most of the time Mt. Hood presents a snowy profile. The dormant volcano is ringed with 11 active glaciers. During the summer, however, after the snow melts from the middle and lower slopes, the mountain shows its rough face: deep and barren glacial troughs, as well as avalanche chutes, wide gray rock fans that unfold between stands of trees. Slopes of loose pumice are sparsely colonized by wind- and cold-stunted subalpine firs and mountain hemlock.

In summertime, the mountain also shows off its more classically beautiful face. The mountain's lower slopes are

Most of the time Mt. Hood presents a snowy profile.

cloaked with dense stands of Douglas fir, accompanied by a rich tangle of undergrowth that includes rhododendron (late-May/June) and huckleberry (ripe and juicy in late August). Alpine meadows such as Paradise Park are gloriously bedecked with wildflowers in July and August: purple Cascade aster, red Indian paintbrush, blue lupine, white avalanche lilies and many more varieties.

Mt. Hood means good skiing (and snowboarding), both during a long winter and a short summer. The mountain's ski potential was recognized early; Magic Mile Chairlift, the nation's second chairlift, was constructed back in 1939.

Mt. Hood means great running; the Hood to Coast relay attracts 17,000 runners and walkers for the annual race from the mountains to the sea. The race is a light-hearted, but taxing road race for most of the recreational runners who compete as teams from clubs, church groups and companies. Nike and Adidas, the two competing athletic shoe companies headquartered in Portland, take the race much more seriously.

Mt. Hood means great climbing; in fact, it's the world's second-most climbed glacier-covered peak (Japan's Mt. Fujiyama is first). Some 10,000 climbers a year tackle various routes up the mountain. One route from Timberline Lodge on the mountain's south side offers the strong hiker (but novice mountaineer) a chance to conquer the summit by joining a pre-dawn expedition led by an experienced guide. Contact the Mt. Hood Recreation Association in Welches for information on climbing guides.

From Timberline Lodge at 6,000-foot elevation, the mountain's most popular ascent begins with a climb to the top of the Palmer Ski Lift, then joins the route known as Hogsback. The memorable 10- to 12-hour round trip climb ascends Palmer Glacier and White River Glacier, passing between Crater Rock and Steel Cliff to the saddle above Crater Rock. The saddle leads to a chute which, in turn, leads to the summit. Safe climbing season is short (May to mid-July).

Timberline Lodge, nothing less than a Pacific Northwest Landmark, is a trailhead for many hiking adventures. The 1930s' creation is a built-to-last structure of massive beams and handsome rock work. It displays the considerable handiwork of the Depression-era Works Progress Administration: hand-forged wrought iron light fixtures, handcrafted furniture, a 92-foot high fireplace, beautiful Pacific Northwest-themed paintings and decor. President Franklin D. Roosevelt dedicated the lodge in 1937, praising it as "a monument to the skills and faithful performance" of WPA workers. You can hear a recording of FDR's speech in the Exhibition Center located on the lodge's main level.

Mt. Hood's long, long winters greatly restricts the activities of the resident mammals, the high-dwelling, whistling, squirrel-like pikas, and those of hikers as well. Some 150 inches of precipitation, mostly in the form of snow, collects on the mountain from October to April; thus the hiking season is quite short. Depending on snowfall and snowmelt, lower trails (below 3,000 feet) are passable around June 1, while higher trails (up to 7,000 feet) can be hiked by mid-July. Hiking season lasts until the end of the September or until the first major snowfall.

Because the hiking season is so brief, the allure of the mountain so great, and the distance from Portland so short, Mt. Hood's pathways are quite popular. And the area's top trails aren't exactly top-secret information to weekending Portlanders. If solitude is what you're seeking, hiking on weekdays or in September will reduce your contact with fellow wilderness users. Check with the Mt. Hood Visitor Center on Highway 26 in Welches and inquire about less-traveled trails in the Zigzag Ranger District.

Timberline Trail is a 40.7-mile, round-the-mountain pathway that tours wildflower-strewn alpine meadows, thick forests, volcanic slopes and deep river canyons. Numerous pathways connect to the Timberline, offering dozens of possible loops and day hiking opportunities. Mt. Hood's hiking season may be short, but there's no shortage of memorable trails on the mountain.

 Mt. Hood's Silcox Hut

Mountaineer Trail

From Timberline Lodge to Silcox Hut is 2 miles round trip with 1,000-foot elevation gain.

Nothing is easy on Mt. Hood, but a small amount of pain and 1,000-foot gain will give you a taste of both the mountain's severity and its hospitality. You can even eliminate some, if not all the pain by riding the Magic Mile Chairlift to this walk's goal, Silcox Hut.

But you don't want to wimp-out do you?

Those hikers opting for the chairlift will join summer skiers on their way to schussing down the Palmer Glacier.

Silcox Hut was built by the Civilian Conservation Corps in 1939, and served for many years as the upper terminal and warming station for the first Magic Mile Chairlift. This lift, only the second built in America, and the first to use steel towers, stayed in service until 1962.

Recently restored, it now serves as an overnight retreat for skiers and hikers. Hot meals are served and bunk-bed style accommodation lodges 24 guests.

Mountaineer Trail is a no-nonsense climb, mostly on a gravel road/cat track. Up top, enjoy the panoramic view of the Cascade Range. For a different return route, you can return downhill on the west side of the chairlift, or head west farther still and pick up a connector trail that descends to the Pacific Crest Trail, 0.75-mile west of Timberline Lodge.

Access: Mountaineer Trail begins at the east side of Timberline Lodge.

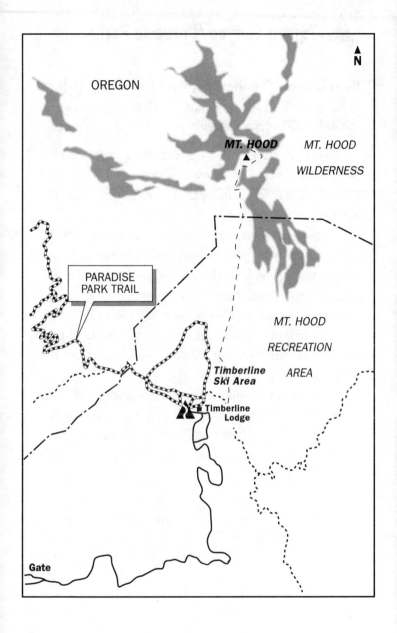

Zigzag Canyon/Paradise Park

Pacific Crest, Timberline, Paradise Park Trails

From Timberline Lodge to Paradise Park is 12.2 miles round trip with 800-foot elevation gain.

Here's Mt. Hood at its best: a dramatic canyon carved by Zigzag River, wildflower-strewn meadows and Cascade vistas that include Three Sisters and Mt. Jefferson.

From Timberline Lodge, you'll head west on Pacific Crest Trail. You'll pass through some handsome meadows, leave lodge guests out for a stroll behind, and a mile out, descend into, then climb out of, Little Zigzag Canyon; this little exercise is but a warm-up to the very severe workout you'll get when you tackle Zigzag Canyon—a knee-jarring descent and lung-popping ascent.

Two and a half miles from the trailhead, catch your breath at a trail intersection and bear right on Paradise Park Trail, which climbs and climbs to the delightful meadows. Get plenty of rest for the return through Zigzag Canyon.

Access: This trail departs from the west side of Timberline Lodge.

 Around Mt. Hood

Timberline Trail

40-mile loop around Mt. Hood; cumulative elevation gain exceeds 9,000 feet.

This trail is a test: of endurance, of sense of direction, of snow-travel skill. It's also a once-in-a-lifetime experience, a look at Mt. Hood from every direction. En route are wildflower-dotted meadows, forests, steep canyons and snowmelt-swollen rushing creeks.

Timberline Trail, like Wonderland Trail around Mt. Rainier and Loowit Trail around Mount St. Helens, circles a great volcano. Constructed in the 1930s by the Civilian Conservation Corps, Timberline Trail is a gem of a trail, at least for the well-prepared backpacker.

Hikers must prepare for Mt. Hood's volatile weather, including sudden storms. An ice-ax—and the mountaineering skills to cross snowfields are helpful. Even when the route is snow-free (as much of it usually is after mid-July) several stretches of trail may fade to obscurity. Map and compass skills are invaluable, especially when weather is bad. The path dips into numerous glacial canyons, where the hiker must cross rushing creeks.

Timberline Lodge is the usual trailhead for the great circle route, most often hiked in a clockwise direction. The lodge, with its showers, swimming pool and many amenities is a great place to end this three- to five-day backpacking trek.

Beginning a westward jaunt from Timberline Lodge, the pass descends to the Zigzag River, then switchbacks up to the glorious meadows of Paradise Park. A switchbacking descent leads to Sandy River at nine miles, nearby camping and Ramona Falls. After reaching trail low point (2,810-foot elevation) the path crosses wide Muddy Fork, the climbs again—Bald Ridge, Eden Park,

Wy East Basin, and on to Elk Cove, at the halfway (20-mile mark). Timberline Trail pushes on to Stranahan Ridge and Cloud Cap Campground, then ascends the rugged slopes of Cooper Spur to path high point (7,320 feet). After traversing snowfields, the trail descends and, during its final 10 miles, alternates between forest and lava country, dipping into and climbing out of many steep ravines. You'll pass under the ski lifts of Mt. Hood Meadows Ski Area, cross the White River and finally link up with the Pacific Crest Trail for the last two miles back to Timberline Lodge.

More than 20 trails branch from Timberline Trail so you're likely to meet and/or follow the path on a day hike on Mt. Hood. For a taste of the Timberline, check out the day hikes to Paradise Park and Cloud Cap described in this book.

Access: The trail begins at Timberline Lodge.

Ramona Falls, Bald Mountain

Ramona Falls, Pacific Crest,
Bald Mountain Trails

*To Ramona Falls is 6.8 miles round trip; to Bald Mountain is
10.5 miles round trip with 1,600-foot elevation gain.*

Some rangers and veteran Mt. Hood hikers say the
jaunt to Ramona Falls is the best and easiest introduction
to the mountain's lower slopes. It's hard to disagree with
this assessment when you spot Ramona Falls, a mossy
series of cascades tumbling down a basalt staircase.

The falls and wet rock walls set in the deep shade of
a grove of towering Douglas fir creates its own microclimate; on hot summer days it can be 15 to 20 degrees
cooler around the falls. Cool, pretty, easy-to-reach—no
wonder the trail to Ramona Falls is so popular with hikers and equestrians. The two new bridges are removed in
late fall, making difficult swift-water crossing.

From Ramona Falls the ambitious can extend their
hike with a loop up and down Bald Mountain (elevation
4,400 feet), which offers excellent views of Mt. Hood.
The only precaution here is that such a loop requires a

Mt. Hood's allure is obvious—from anywhere you stand.

ford of sometimes swift, sometimes too-swift-for-safety Muddy Fork River. Inquire about the river level with local rangers before you try the loop. A second necessary river crossing is accomplished by a bridge.

From road's end, a mellow path meanders by the Sandy River a 3.4 miles to Ramona Falls. While high water crossings are drawbacks to early season hiking, the rhododendrons (late May-June bloomers) are a definite perk.

After savoring the falls, join Pacific Crest Trail for the 5.5-mile climb to Bald Mountain. Remember in mid-ascent you have to cross the Muddy Fork River. Up top, return to the trailhead via the shorter (3-mile-long), but steeper Bald Mountain Trail.

Access: From Highway 26 in the hamlet of Zigzag, some 40 miles east of Portland, turn north on Lolo Pass Road (Forest Service Road 18). This road ascends to postcard-perfect Lost Lake, but five miles along you'll bear right on Forest Service Road 1825, then left on Road 100. Look for the trailhead on the left.

 **Cooper Spur**

Timberline, Cooper Spur Trails

From Cloud Camp Campground to Cooper Spur is 7 miles round trip with 2,500-foot elevation gain

You can't get much higher in Oregon, at least by trail, than 8,514-foot Cooper Spur, which affords excellent vista points from which to eyeball Mt. Hood's impressive glaciers.

This strenuous outing on Mt. Hood's northeast slope, marches from Cloud Cap Campground into the clouds—or at least high above timberline.

Cooper Spur is a spectacular, but extremely exposed part of the mountain. Storms can arise at any time, so keep an eye on the sky and remember your foul weather gear—even in mid-summer.

From the trailhead, join Timberline Trail for a one-mile climb to stone Cooper Spur Shelter and a junction with Cooper Spur Trail. Climb the spur, switchbacking up the steep ridge to the magnificent viewpoint and a trail camp used by summit-bound climbers. Enjoy the inspiring view of the great ice sheets and crevasses of Eliot Glacier, Oregon's largest, as well as a far-reaching panorama of Cascade peaks.

For a little bit different return trip after you've retraced your steps back to Timberline Trail, join Tilly Jane Trail for a descent to another excellent viewpoint, then hike a half-mile uphill back to the campground.

Access: From the junction of highways 26 and 35, head north on the latter road to the west-bound turnoff for Cooper Spur Ski Area. Follow Cooper Spur Road (Forest Road 3510) three miles to Forest Road 3512. Turn left and drive 10 miles on a bumpy, jarring road to Cloud Cap Campground. Look for signed Timberline Trail.

Miles of scenic trails present grand vistas of the mighty Columbia.

COLUMBIA RIVER GORGE

CHAPTER SIX

COLUMBIA GORGE

The Columbia Gorge packs a lot of Oregon into its narrow confines: Pioneer history, epic water projects, boggy rain forests, neat orchards, high desert and high waterfalls.

No wonder Portlanders who have just a day to show visitors the Beaver State's diversity drive east an hour to the Columbia River Gorge National Scenic Area. While the great gorge has an abundance of spectacular scenery, it has a dearth of dining establishments, hotels, or even campgrounds; thus, the gorge is an ideal day trip. (Some eats and accommodations are available at the town of Cascade Locks while amenities abound at Hood River.)

Meandering along the Oregon side of the Columbia River is the Columbia Gorge Scenic Highway. With financing provided by railroad magnate Sam Hill and the backing of prominent Portlanders, highway construction began in 1913 and finished several years later.

Hill, whose highway boosting wasn't completely altruistic (he wanted a road to reach his Maryhill Estate on the Washington side of the river), enlisted the aid of Oregon timber barons, prominent Portlanders and a then-influential national organization called the Good Roads Committee.

Chief engineer Samuel Lancaster studied the great roads of Europe—byways along the Rhine in Germany and through the Alps in Switzerland—before designing his Columbian work of art. Etched into the basalt cliffs, the road offers a beautiful view at every turn.

While few would utter the phrase "the highway builder's art" today without grinning, Lancaster and his crew created a bold asphalt aesthetic: Stunning hairpin turns, scenic turnouts, Florentine-inspired stonework and ornate tunnels.

For years it was the Pacific Northwest's only paved road, as well as America's first officially designated scenic highway.

The public loved the very idea of the road. Civic groups often volunteered their backs and shovels in aid to road crews and convict laborers. After the highway's completion, it was the Sunday drive for Portland families, whose Model Ts crowded the 73-mile route.

Day hikers have enjoyed the gorge for an entire century. Even before completion of the scenic highway, hikers hopped a train to the Bridal Veil stop, pushed up Larch Mountain and down to the tracks again. Steamships also carried hikers to gorge trailheads.

Most gorge trails were built between 1915 and 1924 after completion of the highway. Today some 200 miles of trail penetrate the gorge; most trailheads are within an hour's drive of Portland. Routes range from easy waterfall walks to long, all-day loops into the Columbia Gorge Wilderness.

Most of the gorge's lower elevation footpaths are open all year. Some hikers will even enjoy hiking the gorge in (dare we say characteristic Pacific Northwest weather?) rain and gloom. If there's a break in the clouds, so much the better.

In spring, while the nearby Cascades are still snowbound, the gorge is a green stream of leafy trees. Autumn is awesome when the cottonwood and maple don their fall colors. Leaf peepers will especially admire the dogwood with its peach-red colored leaves.

The Columbia Gorge is more than a natural spectacle; it's a sea-level transportation artery, an 80-mile long, gash in the Cascade Range. The Bonneville Dam and power project tamed the Columbia, one of North America's largest and most powerful rivers (10 times the flow of the Colorado). For a look at river ecology, as the Army Corps of Engineers sees it, and to count the salmon swimming up the fish ladders, stop by the Bonneville Dam Visitor Center.

The Columbia's eight massive hydroelectric dams, so vital to West Coast development, are also fish killers on a grand scale, say environmentalists. In the early nineteenth century, Native American legend said the salmon were so thick you could walk on their backs. Now the salmon numbers are way down, a result of the dams interrupting the fish's spawning and migration journeys, claim a broad spectrum of environmental groups. How to save the salmon—and how much money to spend to preserve this beloved symbol of the Pacific Northwest—will be debated along the banks of the Columbia for many years to come.

For the casual walker, many well-marked short hikes to waterfalls begin from the Columbia Gorge Scenic Highway. Most popular is the short stroll to 620-foot Multnomah Falls.

Three long-distance paths travel the gorge. Gorge Trail, extending 35.5 miles from Bridal Veil to Wyeth is a low elevation, all-year footpath. A few hikers travel it end-to-end, but most use it to connect other trails. A higher elevation gorge trail dips and rises from 4,056-foot Larch Mountain to 4,960-foot Mt. Defiance. The third path is the famed Pacific Crest Trail, which traverses the Columbia Wilderness and crosses the river below Cascade Locks.

 Multnomah Falls

Multnomah Falls Trail

From the base of Multnomah Falls, hike several 3- to 5-mile loops.

Around Multnomah, Oregon's highest waterfall, is a network of trails linking Multnomah and Wahkeena creeks as well as several other notable overlooks. To call the grouping scenic would be understated. The U.S. Forest Service has an information center at Multnomah Lodge at the base of Multnomah Falls and can provide maps and hiking suggestions.

The path is paved to the 620-foot double cascade. From Multnomah Falls, extend your walk with almost innumerable options. With a little creative map-reading, you can put together some splendid three- to five-mile loops that visit several waterfalls. One enjoyable 4.8-mile loop takes in both Multnomah and Wahkeenah falls.

Around Multnomah Falls are not only Columbia Gorge's best developed trails, but the most well-traveled ones, too.

On a sunny weekends hundreds take to the trail, and take family photos with the falls as a backdrop. The viewing platform offers a stunning view of the Columbia River.

One way to beat the crowds is to hike on weekdays or during the off-season, such as in late autumn when the maple and dogwood display their fall colors. Another way to visit Multnomah is to begin your walk at nearby Wahkeenah Falls.

Access: From Interstate 84, take the Multnomah Falls exit (31) and leave your vehicle in the large parking area. Walk through the pedestrian tunnel under the interstate, cross the scenic highway, and follow a signed series of steps and platforms on the east side of the gift shop/visitors center.

 Larch Mountain

Larch Mountain Trail

From Sherrard Point to Larch Mountain is 5.5-mile loop with 1,100-foot elevation gain.

From its rim, Larch Mountain, a small, long-extinct volcano serves up terrific views from its rim of several, much more massive and magisterial volcanoes. To the south soar snowcapped Mount St. Helens and Mt. Jefferson. To the north rise Mount St. Helens, Mt. Adams and Mt. Rainier. And way below, is the wide Columbia flowing westward to the Pacific.

The misnamed mountain has no larch trees (which thrive elsewhere in the Cascade Range) but does boast a grove of old-growth Douglas and noble fir, as well as a curious couple of dwarf junipers clinging to life atop rocky Sherrard Point.

An enjoyable half-day's exploration is the descent into the remnants of Larch Mountain's crater, then a steep climb back to the rim. Another way to go is a one-way descent from Larch Mountain to Multnomah Lodge via Multnomah Falls and the Columbia River Scenic Highway. This knee-jarring but memorable downhiller is regarded by some Columbia connoisseurs as the gorge's most scenic trail. Truly, it's a great hike if you can arrange a car shuttle.

From the summit picnic area, Larch Mountain Trail descends amidst thick forest into the mountain's crater. Two miles out you intersect Trail 444. Follow this path east, crossing Multnomah Creek and joining Trail 424 for the steep climb back up to the picnic area.

Hikers bound for Multnomah Lodge will descend from the first junction 6.8 miles down the handsome gorge of Multnomah Creek, passing several smaller falls before reaching Multnomah Falls. From the bridge across Multnomah you'll descend to the lodge and highway.

Access: From Interstate 84, 22 miles east of Portland, take Exit 22 (Corbett) and connect with Columbia River Scenic Highway. Turn east on Larch Mountain Road and continue 14 miles to road's end and the trailhead at Larch Mountain Picnic Area.

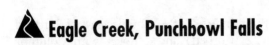 Eagle Creek, Punchbowl Falls

Eagle Creek Trail

From Eagle Creek Road to Punchbowl is 4.2 miles round trip; to 7.5-mile Camp is 15 miles round trip.

For a day hike or a weekend backpack, join Eagle Creek Trail, which begins from the scenic highway a few miles west of the town of Cascade Locks. It's about an hour's walk to well-named Punchbowl Falls. You can continue on the well-engineered path through forest and across the face of cliffs to 7.5-mile Camp for a memorable 15-mile round trip.

Seven waterfalls, small and tall, are highlights of this trail through one of Oregon's most scenic canyons. The not-for-acrophobes trail traverses a sheer rock wall several hundred feet above Eagle Creek and crosses High Bridge over a narrow chasm.

Punchbowl Falls, Louwit Falls and Tunnel Falls (the latter featuring a tunnel carved in the rock behind the falls) are the easy-on-the-eye cascades visited by fairly flat Eagle Creek Trail. A couple of trail camps encourage lingerers to overnight alongside Eagle Creek.

Access: From Interstate 84, take the Eagle Creek Park #41 exit. Follow Eagle Creek Road 0.75 mile to road's end and the parking area.

 **Beacon Rock**

Beacon Rock Trail

To summit of Beacon Rock is 1.6 miles round trip with an 800-foot elevation gain.

For an unforgettable view of the gorge, head for landmark Beacon Rock, a huge hunk of basalt towering 850 feet on the Washington side of the Columbia River a short distance west of Bonneville Dam.

The path climbs moderately south through the woods, then curves east and ascends the rock. Steep switchbacks (made safer by guardrails) and a series of catwalks climb Beacon Rock.

The view—dominated in the foreground by the Bonneville Dam—has no doubt changed considerably since the Lewis and Clark expedition marched past in 1805, and renowned botanist David Douglas collected flora in the area behind Beacon Rock in 1823.

Access: Take the Cascade Locks exit (Exit #44) off eastbound Interstate 84, cross the Columbia River on Bridge of the Gods and double back 7 miles along the Washington side of the river (on SR 14).

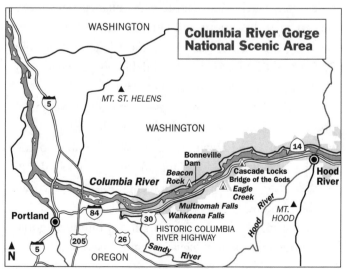

Columbia Gorge

Columbia Gorge Trail

35.5 miles one way.

For the plucky pathfinder, Columbia Gorge Trail is a terrific three-day-or-so odyssey that offers a tour of old-growth forest, dramatic basalt bluffs, a multitude of waterfalls and unrivaled views of the mighty Columbia River. The path, an assemblage of existing hiking trails and newly constructed links, more or less parallels Interstate 84 from Bridal Veil to Wyeth. Even a length of long ago retired Columbia River Highway is incorporated in the trail network.

Columbia Gorge Trail offers a rare-in-these-parts all-year trail. It's snow-free and, if you can time your jaunt between storms, makes a fine winter or spring outing when the many waterfalls en route are in their full glory. Bridal Veil, Multnomah, Triple, Ponytail and Elowah are some of the major falls easily reached by and from the gorge trail.

A second, higher-elevation gorge trail extends 38 miles from Larch Mountain to Mt. Defiance. This more rugged path drops into and climbs out of several steep canyons, traversing the Columbia Wilderness at the 3,000- to 4,000-foot level. You'll definitely get away from it all on this four-day backpacking trip.

Trail activists and greenways promoters have ambitious plans to provide a link of trails all the way from Portland to Hood River. And, perhaps holding to the belief that you can't have too much of a good thing, boosters also wish to establish a length-of-the-gorge trail on the Washington side of the Columbia.

What makes the existing length of Columbia's gorge trail attractive—its low elevation and accessibility—also accounts for its one flaw: it's too close to Interstate 84 and there are times when the roar of traffic overpowers the roar of the waterfalls.

Gorge trail hikers have several options. A three-day, two-night backpacking trip is a good way to go, although campsites are few and far between. Because the lower gorge trail doesn't stray far from Columbia River Scenic Highway, one-way day hikes are a good way to go, provided you arrange a car shuttle. You can fashion a number of loop trips beginning with a walk on lower gorge trail, then using one of the gorge's dozen or so north-south trails to connect with the upper gorge trail. A grand 80-mile loop of both the lower and upper gorge trails would certainly be a hike to remember!

Access: From Interstate 84, take Exit 28 (Bridal Veil) and park in the gravel lot by the Columbia River Highway. The trailhead is across the highway.

Portland's parks and trails are a civic treasure.

PORTLAND

CHAPTER SEVEN

PORTLAND

Portlanders have always been a little bit more eco-oriented than most city-dwellers. Back in 1905 a Portland mayor proposed that alternate streets be razed of their buildings and replaced with trees and the roses so beloved by the local populace. In the early twentieth century, well-to-do landowners bequeathed wooded areas to the city on the condition that no wheeled vehicle ever violate the sanctity of these preserves.

Portland decided to emphasize its land, not its port, forsaking its opportunity to become a big-time player in the emerging global economy and Pacific Rim trade. Instead, the city marshalled its considerable resources, natural and human, to pursue the goal of making this most bountiful land the most livable it could be.

It cheerfully decided to take second-place to Seattle as the Pacific Northwest's commercial capital and opted for a home-grown Portland-style prosperity. The traditional measurements of big-city success are present—a deep-water harbor, convention center, diverse cultural venues and all the amenities—but a commitment to Portland as a place to live (not just work) is of the utmost importance to its citizenry.

Located at the confluence of the Columbia and Willamette rivers, Portland is situated about 90 miles from the Pacific Ocean and 50 miles from the Cascade Range. Behind the compact metropolis rise the park-filled West Hills, an inspiring green backdrop for the central city's small collection of skyscrapers. Views are awesome from the West Hills over the city and its rivers out to 11,235-foot Mt. Hood and surrounding snow-topped Cascade peaks.

In a bold move that still has the nation's city planners nodding in admiration, Portland demolished a freeway that extended along the Willamette's west bank and replaced it with Tom McCall Waterfront Park. The former four-lane blossomed into a two-mile greenbelt of lawns, trees and a grand riverfront promenade.

Not only was the riverfront cleaned up, so was the river. Twentieth century industrial developments and discharges had wrecked what had been a popular recreation area and vital wildlife habitat. Proof of the river's recovery is in the trout and salmon that swim by and the waterfront anglers that try to hook them.

In the early 1970s the city also declared war on suburban sprawl. While most western cities chose to grow like Los Angeles and Phoenix by absorbing outlying areas, Portland voters elected a regional government that exercised strict development control over a three-county, 24-city area. Rather than hyper or haphazard development, some new projects feature creative mixed use (residential and commercial) projects, the downtown area has been restored, and there is plenty of public transit.

Some of the aspects that make Portland one of the nation's most livable cities also make it one of the most walk-able.

Portland's commitment to a green city continues. Some proud local conservationists claim that Portland has more urban wilderness than any other city in the nation—nearly 200 parks and wildlife refuges. These parks range from giant 4,800-acre Forest Park, America's largest wooded city park, to Mill Ends Park, with a 24-inch-wide measurement that has earned it a listing in the *Guinness Book of World Records* as the smallest city park in the United States.

Portland's parks offer panoramic views. Council Crest, the city's high point, offers both metropolitan and

Cascade Range vistas. Another great vista is from a near-by extinct volcano, Mt. Tabor, believed to be the nation's only extinct volcano located within a city.

Portland is pedestrian-friendly for many reasons—among them the greenery of its parks and West Hills, and the relative compactness of its urban attractions.

Downtown measures just 13 by 26 blocks. These city blocks are oh-so-short by New York standards, meaning the city walker can easily crisscross the city in a day. Sidewalks are wide and small parks with benches are plentiful. Making exploration easier still is MAX, the city's light rail system, and Tri-Met buses, both of which are free of charge in the downtown area, known as Fareless Square.

Pointing walkers in the right direction are pairs of Portland Guides. Clad in kelly-green baseball caps and jackets and blue pants, these hosts afoot can answer any where to go, how to go, when to go question you might have.

Best city walk—at least the most complete one—is outlined in a free map/guide offered by Powell's Bookstore (1005 W. Burnside Street), one of the west's great independent booksellers. The bookstore's suggested ambitious seven-mile sojourn can be shortened to suit one's time and energy.

City-strollers should definitely tour the Skidmore Historic District, Portland's old downtown with buildings dating from the 1880s. Prevailing architecture is built-to-last brick with cast-iron facades and Italianate interpretation. A good place to begin is the bronze and granite Skidmore Fountain, long time rest-stop for horses and humans.

In recent years the city has decreed that one percent of the cost of every new building must be spent on pub-lic art. The Regional Arts and Culture Council (309 S.W. Sixth Ave, Suite 100) offers a brochure that suggests a walking tour that visits more than three dozen works of art. Not surprisingly these public art projects have Northwest themes. *Allow Me*, located in Pioneer Courthouse Square, is a bronze sculpture of a man carrying an umbrella.

And naturally, in this city of greenery, the public art has an eco-emphasis. Check out *Portlandia* in front of the Portland Building and observe *Earth Mother* kneeling, trident in hand. Then there's block-long (South West Clay Street) Ira Keller Memorial Fountain, which depicts the Pacific Northwest's many creeks and cascades.

Some walkers prefer the tamer terrain of the International Rose Test Garden in Washington Park where more than 519 rose varieties blossom. Since 1907, Portland has held an annual early June Rose Festival, championing its "City of the Roses" nickname.

Other walkers go wild on the 14-mile long Wildwood Trail. Not surprisingly (for Portland), the trail had its origins in the early 1900s when famed landscape architect brothers Frederick and John Olmsted came to landscape the fairgrounds for the 1905 Lewis and Clark Exposition and left behind an ambitious park plan and a proposal for a 40-mile loop trail through Forest Park and around a greenbelt.

Portland's 40-Mile Loop Land Trust is working to complete the project, as well as another hundred miles of connecting pathways that link parks along the Columbia and Willamette rivers.

 Tom McCall Waterfront Park

Waterfront Promenade

From Riverplace to Steel Bridge is 1.75 miles one way.

How often have we walkers witnessed greenery vanish under four lanes of asphalt or seen a neighborhood bisected then destroyed by a freeway?

Too many instances of paradise-paving to count, right?

Now how often do we walkers get to see where a freeway was plowed under and replaced by a park?

Probably only in Portland.

Back in the late 1960s, Oregon Governor Tom McCall and Portland conservationists envisioned a greenway, not a freeway, along the west bank of the Willamette River. That vision, de-evolution by design, became a reality with Tom McCall Waterfront Park, a 1.75-mile long park and promenade.

With the freeway long gone, the only traffic along the river is foot traffic. The once-constant roar of cars and trucks has been replaced by the soothing strains of the Oregon Symphony's regularly scheduled summer outdoor concerts.

A walk along the Willamette River is a journey into the city's history. This river connects the city with the Columbia River and the Pacific Ocean. The Willamette, thanks to a three decade-long cleanup effort is now a

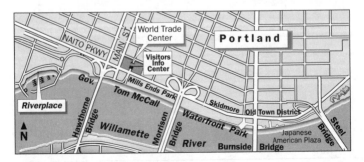

viable habitat for trout and salmon, and an increasingly popular destination for water sports enthusiasts.

From the south end of Waterfront Park, a concrete promenade winds along the river bank. A pedestrian's progress is marked by the many bridges en route: Hawthorne Bridge, Morrison Bridge (once a wooden structure, and the first to span the Willamette in 1887), Burnside Bridge, under which Portland's famed Saturday Market is held, and finally Steel Bridge.

Urban adventurers could return through the city's Skidmore Historic District. On the way back walkers can cross busy Naito Parkway (formerly Front Avenue) at Salmon Street to pop into the Portland Oregon Visitors Association's Visitor Information Center. And (carefully) check out Mill Ends Park, "America's smallest city park," located in the middle of Naito Parkway at Taylor Street, a block north of the visitors center.

Access: Begin this walk at the RiverPlace development on Naito Parkway at SW Montgomery Street. Park at the pay lot at this corner or compete for one of the metered spaces along nearby streets.

By bus: Tri-Met buses make frequent stops along Naito Parkway. Walk down to the Willamette waterfront from the nearest stop.

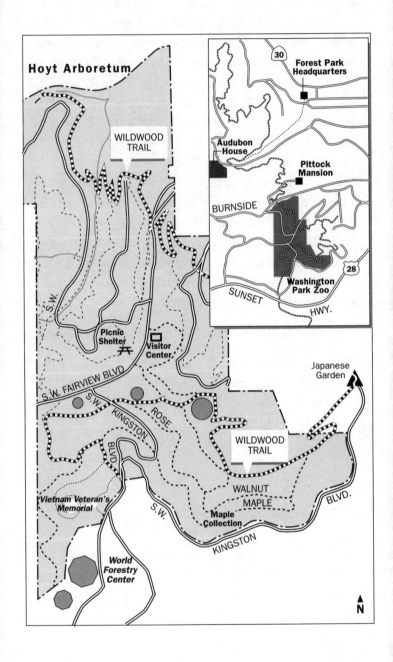

Hoyt Arboretum

WILDWOOD
TRAIL

Picnic
Shelter

Visitor
Center

S.W. FAIRVIEW BLVD.

S.W. KINGSTON

ROSE

BLVD.

Vietnam Veteran's
Memorial

S.W.

WILDWOOD
TRAIL

Japanese
Garden

WALNUT
MAPLE

Maple
Collection

BLVD.

KINGSTON

World
Forestry
Center

N

Forest Park
Headquarters

30

Audubon
House

Pittock
Mansion

BURNSIDE

SUNSET

HWY.

28

Washington
Park Zoo

Washington Park

Wildwood National Recreation Trail

From Washington Park's International Rose Test Garden to the World Forestry Center is 4 miles round trip; to Pittock Mansion is 4 miles round trip.

Portland's Washington Park is an attractive combination of nature trails, garden paths and some must-see natural and historical attractions. It's that rare park that manages to merge such different attractions as picnic areas, nature trails, a zoo, tennis courts and renowned rose garden with style and grace.

Perched in the hills high above downtown and the Willamette River, Washington Park, along with adjoining Forest Park and Hoyt Arboretum, form the largest municipal parkland within an American city. The park, established in 1871, has its share of auto traffic, but also boasts many tranquil places linked by a spider web of trails. Near the beginning of this walk is the International Rose Test Garden, particularly attractive between June to October when more than 7,000 rose bushes bloom.

Wildwood National Recreation Trail is a 26.3-mile path extending from Washington Park to the northern end of Forest Park. Walk the trail in a weekend or combine short segments of Wildwood with other attractive footpaths and (closed) service roads to create loops of three to five miles or more.

From Washington Park, hikers can follow Wildwood Trail to the World Forestry Center and/or Pittock Mansion. The Forestry Center's 70-foot "Talking Tree" offers a good introduction to the museum, which also has many attractive exhibits that highlight the recreational and educational uses of forestry. Two more engaging exhibits are "Forests of the World," a memorable multimedia show and "Tillamook Burn," a push-button pre-

Wildwood Trail explores Washington Park's leafy splendor.

sentation of a dreadful 1930s' forest fire that blackened one of Oregon's coastal regions. My favorite interactive exhibit explores the modern-day forest planning process and lets the budding bureaucrat make land-use decisions while hearing advice from various special interest groups.

In 1853 young printer's apprentice Henry Pittock came to Portland; in a mere eight years he rose to editor of *The Oregonian*, then, and still, the state's most influential newspaper. In 1908 he began construction of his 16,000-square foot, top-of-the hill chateau, furnished in Victorian and French Renaissance styles. Guided tours (fee) of Pittock Mansion, offered most afternoons from noon to 4 P.M., provide an insight into Portland's growth and development. The mansion's balconies and gardens offer commanding views of the city.

Walk up a gravel path, then ascend on the switch-backing Japanese Garden Trail, climbing first through an exotic landscape dominated by English ivy then pass through a more typical Northwest scene of Oregon grape, sword fern, Douglas fir and western hemlock. High above the Japanese Garden is the junction with Wildwood Trail.

Go left on Wildwood Trail to reach the World Forestry Center. You'll pass plenty of alternate pathways as you work your way to the Oregon Vietnam Veterans Living Memorial, then over to the sprawling cedar shingle-roofed World Forestry Center building. With a park map (available at the forestry center) you can improvise an alternate return route.

Go right on Wildwood Trail to reach Pittock Mansion. You'll cross a couple paved roads and encounter lots of native California trees—giant sequoias and coastal redwoods—on your way to the mansion. Wildwood Trail continues far into Forest Park if you feel so inclined.

Access: Follow West Burnside Street to Tichner Street into Washington Park. Head south on S.W. Tichner Street and follow the signs for the Japanese Garden. Best parking is just above the International Rose Test Garden by the tennis courts. Begin your walk at a sign and gateway for the Japanese Garden opposite the tennis courts.

 **Council Crest**

Marquam Nature Trail

From Marquam Nature Park to Council Crest is 4 miles round trip with 900-foot elevation gain.

The Native American leaders who convened councils high on this hilltop must have taken inspiration from the commanding views afforded them. Today, clear-day views from atop Council Crest remain inspiring. The reward for the climb to the city's 1,070-foot high point is a panorama of Cascade peaks including Mt. Rainier, Mount St. Helens and Mt. Hood. Much closer vistas of downtown Portland and sprawling-to-infinity Beaverton are also part of the crest view.

Back in the early 1900s, a streetcar clattered up Council Crest, carrying pleasure-seekers to an amusement park, complete with roller-coaster and dance hall. Nowadays its foot-power, not electric power, that gets you to the top, where a fine picnic spot awaits.

The path is part of Portland's 40-Mile Loop. Combine this trail with others to walk north to Forest Park or south and east to the Willamette River and the city.

The path climbs through a thick forest of Douglas fir, big-leaf maple and red alder. At times the zigzagging, fern-lined trail leaves civilization far behind; other stretches meander near hillside homes and cross three mountain roads.

Learn more about Council Crest history and ecology at trailhead displays in Marquam Nature Park.

Access: From S.W. 6th Ave, follow S.W. Sam Jackson Road. Make a right on S.W. Marquam Court and leave your car in Marquam Nature Park's small two-hour lot. This walk begins on signed Sam Jackson Trail.

 **Powell Butte**

Mountain View, Wildhorse Trails

To crest of Powell Butte is a 3-mile loop.

For those in the know, it's Portland's volcano.

True, Powell Butte (elevation 630 feet) lacks the stature and name recognition of nearby landmark volcanoes Mt. Hood and Mount St. Helens, but this now-quiet volcanic mound does offer a pleasant excursion and some great metropolitan views. From the butte's summit are great views of those big-time volcanoes, as well as downtown Portland, Mt. Adams and Mt. Jefferson.

Powell Butte is the centerpiece of a city park located in southeast Portland. Quiet cows and noisy motorcycle riders used the butte until the Portland Parks and Recreation Department took over a few years back.

Powell's slopes are shaded with Douglas fir and big-leaf maple, accompanied by tangles of thimbleberry and thickets of poison oak. Wild roses peep out from the underbrush.

Depending on your time and inclination, you can make a bee-line for the summit on 0.6-mile long Mountain View Trail or fashion a more circuitous route via Wildhorse Trail, Mt. Hood Trail or Meadowland Trail, in addition to a couple more. In all, nine miles of trail weave through the park.

Atop Powell Butte is a former orchard of pear, apple, and walnut trees, as well as Summit Orchard Picnic Area.

Access: From Portland, follow Interstate 205 east and exit on Powell Boulevard. Drive three miles east on Southeast Powell Boulevard to 162nd Avenue. The entrance road to Powell Butte's parking lot is at SE Powell Boulevard and 162nd Avenue.

 Sauvie Island

Warrior Rock Trail
To top of Sauvie Island is 7 miles round trip

Birds, blackberries and beaches are the highlights of a walk on Sauvie Island, a 16-mile rural retreat and wildlife refuge located near the confluence of the Willamette and Columbia rivers.

The southern half of Sauvie Island is fertile farmland, created by silt deposited by the Columbia River. Pumpkin patches and berry bushes are plentiful on the island, as are U-pick'em farms and roadside produce stands.

The northern half of the island is the wild side, an Oregon Department of Fish and Wildlife-administered wetland of lakes and marshes, prime habitat for more than 250 bird species. Hundreds of thousands of migratory ducks and geese rest and feed on the island in autumn and winter. Bald eagles, sandhill cranes and great blue herons frequent the island.

Laurent Sauvie, a mid-nineteenth century French Canadian dairyman gave the island his name. Cows still graze island meadows and are often encountered on the path to Warrior Rock. The trail leads three miles to the Warrior Rock Lighthouse, once operated by the Coast Guard. The lighthouse is now off limits, but an enticing beach is nearby and the hiker can continue another half-mile to the top of the island, where there are some excellent picnicking areas and good views of the passing boat traffic. (On sunny days, the beach is often clothing-optional.)

Walkers can choose to follow an occasionally cow-pie-splattered road lined with willows and black cottonwood or slosh through the sand and mud right alongside the river.

Access: From Portland, head 10 miles west on Highway 30 to Sauvie Island Bridge. Turn right and proceed north on NW Sauvie Island Road. Turn right again on Reeder Road and follow it 12.5 miles, first to the east side of the island, then north along the island's shore. Reeder Road (gravel beyond Walton Beach) deadends at a parking lot. Step over a hikers' stile to join the trail.

WASHINGTON

Devastation from the 1980 eruption of Mount St. Helens is still very evident.

MOUNT ST. HELENS

CHAPTER EIGHT

MOUNT ST. HELENS
NATIONAL VOLCANIC MONUMENT

Not so long ago it was a perfect cone, a long dormant volcano. Pre-blast Mount St. Helens was the jewel of the Cascades, an inviting destination for anglers, hikers and campers. The mountain, along with Spirit Lake and the surrounding backcountry of Gifford Pinchot National Forest was the pride of Washington.

Everything changed on May 18, 1980 when this sleeping beauty awoke with a start. Apparently, the native Klickitat who called the peak Tahonelatclah ("Fire Mountain") had it right all along.

The top of the mountain was part of the largest landslide in history, replaced by a hole two miles long and one mile wide. Mount St. Helens didn't exactly blow its top, though; it was a lateral blast (more destructive than a vertical one because no energy is dissipated overcoming gravity). Hot gases and debris, propelled outward at speeds exceeding 200 miles per hour. Debris—pebbles, boulders, silt and truck-sized hunks of glacial ice—raced down into Spirit Lake, raising the water level by 200 feet. A majority of avalanche-dislodged debris swept rapidly (13 miles in about 10 minutes) down the North Fork of Toutle River.

An awesome 680 degrees F. blast cloud—atomized pieces of mountain, hot gases and organic material— moved at speeds up to 250 miles per hour. Hot muddy liquid choked rivers. Mudflows engulfed forests.

The eruption drastically altered the ecosystem to say the least, covering 24 square miles with mud, debris and volcanic rock. Many more square miles became a desert of ash. Nearby forests were flattened. Ash darkened the skies and blanketed towns as far away as Yakima, 80 miles distant.

What you saw depended on where you stood and who you are. Loggers saw much timber lost but millions of board feet available to salvage.

The military mind saw a land "bombed" with the equivalent of 400 million tons of TNT or 300 Hiroshima-sized nuclear weapons.

Seismologists pointed to the 5.1 magnitude earth-quake that caused the mountain's bulging north face to collapse. Economists estimated eruption-caused damages totaled $1.5 billion.

Wildlife biologists put the death toll at thousands of fish killed when water temperatures rose to the boiling point. Whole herds of elk, deer and mountain goats were wiped out.

Meteorologists suggested the blast may have been responsible for climatic changes as far away as Europe.

Although it seemed like complete and total annihila-tion of the biosphere it wasn't. Much vegetation that fate-ful May day was under the cover of snow. In fact, the land is recovering quite remarkably from the big blow. What was black and gray is now dark green and light. New vegetation quite literally sprang from the ashes— beginning a process biologists call recolonization. First the hardy fire weed pioneers the way, followed by this-tles, ferns and berry bushes. Eventually, even the conifer forests will regenerate.

Animal life, too, has returned. Hibernating frogs and salamanders, lying dormant under the mud, survived the eruption. Beaver have been sighted in Spirit Lake. Every amphibian and reptile represented before the eruption has since returned.

After the eruption, tourism exploded, too. Appar-ently more travelers are drawn to a landscape that now more resembles the Inferno than Paradise.

In 1982, some 110,000 acres were set aside by Congress as Mount St. Helens National Volcanic Monument and placed under the stewardship of the U.S. Forest Service. A network of scenic highways, and two major visitor centers were built to serve the needs of the more than one million visitors a year who are drawn to the scene of the natural disaster.

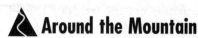 Around the Mountain

Loowit Trail

Around Mount St. Helens is a 28-mile loop.

Walking up to it is inspiring, walking up it is breath-taking. But walking around it is the best way to appreciate Mount St. Helen's diverse ecologies, as well as the magnitude of the cataclysmic events that took place May 18, 1980.

Loowit Trail circles the volcano, a marathon-length exploration of nature's devastation and subsequent regeneration, as well as a tour of old-growth forests and lands untouched by the mountain's fire storms. The contrasts between what the eruption hit and missed are startling. Witnessing the flora recolonizing and wildlife returning in the blast area is quite life affirming.

The path is named for a lovely and no doubt temperamental native maiden who long ago was transformed into a mountain. Loowit Trail is a three-act play: First, a close-up look at past tragic events, next a look at life touched by, but not overwhelmed by natural disaster, and finally a return to the devastating scene, this time with the promise of recovery and the assurance that life does indeed go on.

Adding (if any addition is needed) to Loowit Trail's feeling of remoteness is its route, which does not meet a road. However, a half-dozen or more footpaths lead from roads to connect with the trail.

Best place to join Loowit Trail is from the Windy Ridge trailhead. You start with an incomparable panorama of the crater before beginning your counterclockwise contour around the mountain.

The path, as depicted on the National Monument map, does not appear to be all that difficult; meandering around the mountain between the 3,500- and 4,700-foot elevation level. But the map is not the territory. Loowit Trail traverses joint-jarring fields of lava blocks, and dips in and out of a dozen ravines. The trail requires mushing through soft sand and ash as tiring as soft Sahara dunes.

Not only is Loowit Trail brutal on the body, it's rough on equipment too. Gritty volcanic ash can damage camp stoves, water purification filters, cameras and binoculars.

From Windy Ridge, Truman Trail connects via windy trail #216 E to Loowit Trail, which crosses pumice slopes between the great yawning crater and Spirit Lake, and offers vistas of a vast ashy wasteland. Beyond the Pumice Plains the path ascends out of the blast zone, weaving between scorched and untouched forest to Crescent Ridge. After many more ups and downs the path, flirting with timberline, reaches a junction with Butte Camp Trail about halfway around the mountain. A 1.25-mile steeply descending detour leads to the camp.

The second half of Loowit Trail is even more diffi-cult—brutal walking over old lava flows, and the head-water canyons cut by Muddy River and Pine Creek. The final four miles across the Plains of Abraham are a bit more mellow, and a time to savor the considerable accomplishment of a circumlocution of the mountain.

Plains of Abraham

Plains of Abraham Trail
From Windy Ridge to the Plains of Abraham is 8.2 miles round trip.

Even before the 1980 eruption, the Plains of Abraham were barren, forlorn and treeless—the result of periodic avalanches sweeping down the slopes of Mount St. Helens.

With the eruption, more earthly chaos befell the plains. A huge lahar (an Indonesian word that scientists use to describe a thick soup of sand, gravel, mud and water) engulfed the plain and spilled into nearby Ape Canyon. And as if this massive mudflow was not sufficient destruction, airborne pumice shelled the Plains of Abraham, giving them their present moonscape appearance.

Views of the devastated area from the Windy Ridge trailhead are awesome and a preview of the pathway to come. The path crosses stark slopes on the blast zone's edge before arriving at the north end of the Plains of Abraham. The trail then edges along the east side of the half-mile wide, mostly lifeless plains.

With the right equipment and precautions, hikers can explore scenes of volcanic devastation.

125

Ape Canyon Trail junction is where most day hikers call it a day, but if shuttle arrangements have been made, you could hike the 5.5 miles crossing the head of Ape Canyon to the Road 83 parking area for Ape Canyon. The canyon, named for a sighting of the legendary Bigfoot in the 1920s, is a mix of mudflows and an old-growth forest of Douglas fir and noble fir.

An interesting option for the return trip is to sample a little bit of Loowit Trail, the spectacular 28-mile around-the-mountain pathway. At the north end of the Plains of Abraham, veer leftward on Loowit Trail. The views and the pathway itself are worth the extra half-mile distance and 600-foot elevation gain on the ascent back to Windy Ridge.

Access: From Road 25, eight miles south of Randle, turn west onto Road 26 and proceed 15 miles to Road 99. Turn west and drive to road's end, the trailhead and Windy Ridge interpretive center.

Mount St. Helens Summit

Ptarmigan Trail and
Monitor Ridge climbing route

To the summit is 9.5 miles round trip with 4,600-foot eleva-tion gain.

Mount St. Helens' once-symmetrical cone is now a shattered crater surrounded by steep, barren ridges. A climb to the lip of the crater offers a firsthand look at the effects of the volcano's 1980 eruption and of blasts from the distant past.

In 1987, Mount St. Helens' south side was reopened, offering climbers the opportunity to conquer a mountain now 1,313 feet lower than the original summit. From the crater rim, you can look out at the lava dome and try to imagine the cataclysmic events that took place here.

Climbers Bivouac, because it offers a fairly high headstart at 3,700 feet is Climbers Bivouac. "Climbers" is the key word here; more than half the route up St. Helens is trail-less.

The ascent begins with a two-mile hike through the forest on Ptarmigan Trail. From timberline, the way to the top is via Monitor Ridge over steep pumice and lava slopes. The ridge route is waymarked with wooden posts. Be sure to watch your step on the unstable, land-slide-prone crater rim.

Mount St. Helens is not a technically difficult climb, but it is one that requires a degree of doggedness and ample preparation. Such preparation should include wraparound sunglasses or goggles, sunscreen and foul weather apparel. Gaiters are invaluable, both for sloshing through melting snow and piles of ash. Depending on the year's snowfall, crampons and an ice ax are often nec-essary well into the summer climbing season.

The Forest Service limits the number of Mount St.

Helens climbers to 100 per day. A climbing permit ($15 per person) is required. Reservations (highly encouraged during the summer to avoid disappointment) can be made by writing to the National Monument or in person at national monument headquarters near Amboy.

Forty unreserved climbing permits per day are available by lottery from Jack's Restaurant and Store, located on Highway 503, some five miles west of Cougar. Here's the drill: Sign-in begins at 5:30 P.M. Permits are issued at 6:00 P.M.

Permits are good for 24 hours. All climbers are required to sign in and out at the climber's register outside Jack's before and after a climb.

Allow an entire day (8 to 10 hours) for the climb to the crater and back.

Climb this volcano for a firsthand look at the great blast of 1980.

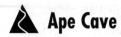 Ape Cave

Through Lower Cave is 0.5-mile one way; through Upper Cave is 1.5 miles with a 1.25-mile return trail.

In a National Monument full of "novelty hikes" Ape Cave is the surely the most unusual. Here's your chance to step into the dark recesses of North America's longest intact lava tube. Prowl the pitch black corridors of the 12,810-foot cave, picking your way over volcanic rubble and passing beneath the perennial crowd pleaser—a huge hunk of lava known as the "meatball" wedged into the cave's ceiling.

Actually, more than 50 lava tubes are located in the long basalt flow on Mount St. Helen's south side; however, these caves contain fragile geological formations as well as unusual plant and animal assemblages. Neither the Forest Service nor scientists want to publicize these locations. The Forest Service refers compulsive cave explorers to local spelunking groups for more information and excursions.

Ape Cave was created when downhill-flowing molten lava cooled and hardened on the outside while the remaining hot liquid inside continued moving, leaving behind a tube.

Ape Cave was first discovered in 1947 by a logger who observed a tree that had toppled into the cave mouth. Follow-up exploration was accomplished by a 1950s outdoors club known as The Mount St. Helen's Apes, who named the cave.

Ape Cave may be a tourist attraction, but credit the Forest Service for its admirable restraint in developing the area. Ape Cave has no improvements except a couple of metal staircases at the entrances and is a refreshing change from the privately owned, electrically lit tourist traps located elsewhere in the West.

The lower cave, which extends some 4,000 feet downslope, is fairly easy walking on a sand floor and offers photo opportunities of the famed lava meatball. The upper cave, which slopes upward 8,000 feet, has trickier footing over some rock rubble.

Return from the upper cave underworld via Ape Cave Trail, which tours an old lava flow of ropy, Hawaiian-style lava known as pahoehoe. The path visits a pleasant old-growth forest as well as a dead one, suffocated by a mudflow resulting from Mount St. Helens' 1980 eruption.

Access: From Road 90 in Cougar drive 7 miles north to a junction with Road 83, following this road 3 miles, then turning left on Road 8303, for a final mile to Ape Cave. Remember to bring flashlights for this hike, or rent a gas lamp from the Forest Service Information Station.

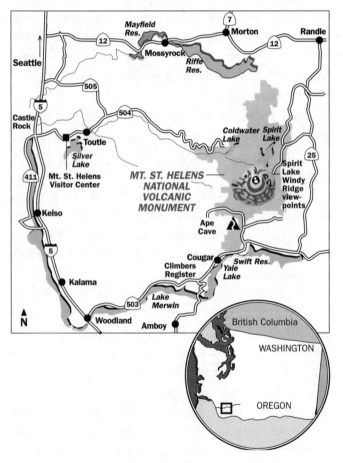

 Spirit Lake

Harmony Trail

From Harmony Viewpoint to Spirit Lake is 2 miles round trip.

The old photos show the beauty of this place: calm, crystal-clear Spirit Lake, dramatic Harmony Falls tumbling from a nearby mountainside, a lodge and happy campers. Rising above this storybook setting was a classic, snow-capped alpine peak—Mount St. Helens.

The modern photographer sees an altogether different scene through the viewfinder. An avalanche triggered by the volcano's 1980 eruption plunged into the lake, raising the water level by more than 200 feet. Monster waves surged as much as 800 feet against the ridges above the lake. As the waves and water level receded, trees blown down by the blast were dumped into the lake, there to float in what came to resemble a giant millpond. Post-blast, Spirit Lake swelled to twice its original size and occupied a different lakebed too—a one-time old-growth forest.

In the weeks before Mount St. Helens erupted, colorful Harry Truman, for a half-century the manager of Spirit Lake Lodge, became a national celebrity when he refused the pleas of authorities who urged him to evacuate Spirit Lake. Today, Truman lies buried beneath hundreds of feet of avalanche debris at the bottom of the recast Spirit Lake.

From Harmony Falls Viewpoint, the trail switchbacks down through a fallen forest. The trees—logs now—all fell like so many matchsticks in the same direction away from the volcano's crater.

One-time scenic attraction Harmony Falls was shortened by half by eruption earth movements and is now but a shadow of its former self. The trail ends at the ash- and rock-strewn lakeshore.

Access: From Road 99, 3.7 miles before road's end at Windy Ridge Viewpoint, park at the Harmony Viewpoint.

Seattle landmarks: The 605-foot Space Needle, 14,411-foot Mt. Rainier.

9

SEATTLE

CHAPTER NINE

SEATTLE

The Pacific Northwest's primary colors—green, gray and blue—are Seattle's colors. Green hues are those of the bountiful evergreen forests on the city's edge. Gray is the sky over Seattle; the city's rainy weather, ranging in intensity from mists to monsoons, is infamous. Blue waters surround the "Emerald City," which occupies a narrow strip of land between Puget Sound and 18-mile long Lake Washington.

North of downtown are canals and Lake Union, which bisects Seattle. Boats and bridges are crucial to the city's transportation system, as most commuters cross water on their way to work.

From this city built on hills, views of big and bold mountains fill the horizon. To the west are the Olympic Mountains, to the east are the snowy summits of the Cascade Range dominated by Mt. Rainier, referred to by locals simply as "The Mountain."

This geography of waters deep and mountains high contributes to the clean and green lifestyle of Seattle citizens, a way of life that's a source of civic pride. Residents exchange briefcases for backpacks, cell phones for fly rods with the greatest of ease and, rain or shine, head for the great outdoors.

Manhattan-shaped Seattle bears some surface resemblance to several cities, including northern neighbor and Pacific Rim rival, Vancouver. Seattle, sometimes compared to San Francisco, has an extensive bayfront, is constructed on hills and has a Pacific Rim orientation in art, culture and commerce. Some complain Seattle has too often followed a Los Angeles-like development pattern, complete with a freeway through the heart of the city and sprawling suburbs. Pugetopolis, as it's sometimes known, now numbers some three million people.

Its resemblance to other places aside, Seattle moves at its own pace, slowed in part by the frequent rains. It's not so much the sheer volume of rain (annual precipitation is often less than 60 inches and averages a surprisingly low 36.2 inches) it's the number of rainy days: measurable rainfall is recorded 150 to 180 days a year.

Helping to pick up the civic pace are an astonishing number of espresso-selling establishments. On the Seattle waterfront, you can get java from a drive-through stand or from the waterside McDonald's. You can't walk a city block without seeing a sign offering coffee for sale. For those walkers who like a caffeine buzz, the hometown of Starbuck's is a great place to stroll.

Seattle became the original high-tech city in 1916, when William Boeing began building airplanes. Boeing Aircraft became the largest employer in the Pacific Northwest. The still-futuristic-looking Space Needle, built in 1962 when Seattle hosted the World's Fair, seems to symbolize the city's confidence in the techno-future. Software giant Microsoft, and a multitude of smaller computer-related companies are part of today's high-tech corporate culture.

Before Seattle became high-tech it was rough-neck. Loggers chopped down the evergreens that surrounded the city and dragged them down the city's slopes to Henry Yesler's sawmill near the harbor. What is now Yesler Way was then known as Skid Road. In later years the road attracted brothels, bars and down-and-outers; it was misnamed "Skid Row" by East Coast newspapermen and soon seedy districts in cities across America became known as skid rows. Still, somewhat oddly, Seattle claims the first Skid Row.

Downtown Seattle is best explored on foot and by availing oneself of bus service (free in the downtown zone, low-cost in the outlying areas). A quarter-century long building boom has given Seattle a mostly bland skyline of skyscrapers that, though impressive when viewed from a harbor ferry, is of only passing interest to the explorer afoot. Seattle's best city-walking is in two older and more colorful areas—Pike Place Market, the nation's foremost farmers market, and Pioneer Square, the city's restored old-town.

Pike Place Market, located at the bottom of Pike Street, opened in 1907 when farmers brought their produce directly from the fields to the people. The low-cost market especially thrived during the 1930s Depression, but fell on hard times in the 1960s. Seattle citizens rallied to save their market in the 1970s, and today the labyrinth of produce stands, eateries and craft stalls is the city's number one tourist attraction.

From the market, intrepid city-walkers can follow stairs and a route known as Hill Climb past more shops down to the waterfront. Seattle's shore is mostly a working port, interspersed with some restaurants and shops.

Pioneer Square, which preserves some of Seattle's oldest buildings, is the other can't-miss city walk. Before the turn of the century, this low-lying part of town often reeked when the sewer system, dependent on tidal flushing, backed up. The ingenious solution to the problem was to raise the street level; however, this re-engineering put the ground floors of Seattle's best buildings underground. These various buildings, connected by tunnels and corridors, soon attracted unsavory characters and illegal activities such as drinking during the Prohibition era. Seattle's secret passageways were restored during the 1960s and can be explored on an entertaining 90-minute guided walk. The Underground Tours depart every hour or so from Doc Maynard's Tavern on First Avenue.

Walkers who like their scenery green will find much to explore in the parks and wilderness areas just outside Pugetopolis. Ancient forests, dramatic waterfalls, and inspiring vistas are located within a short drive of Seattle. If local conservationists have their way, many of these scenic attractions will soon be accessible by trail, too. A proposed Mountains to Sound Greenway, located near Puget Sound's Interstate 90 corridor, will link dozens of scenic attractions with a recreation trail. Such a trail will be a fitting link between the city and its wilderness origins and be popular with its citizens and visitors alike, many of whom were drawn here by the city's proximity to the wild.

Washington State ferries depart Seattle for several walker-friendly destinations, including Bainbridge Island.

 Discovery Park

Discovery Park Nature Loop
2.8 miles round trip.

Seattle's largest park is laced with an extensive network of beach and blufftop trails. Semi-wild, 535-acre Discovery Park, strategically located between the city's urban/suburban edge and Puget Sound is a green sanctuary of meadows and second-growth forest.

In 1792, Puget Sound explorer Captain George Vancouver sailed by in his vessel, the HMS *Discovery*, from which the park takes its name. A century later, the U.S. Army established Fort Lawton, a small military reservation with housing and a parade ground. Seattle's sewers arrived soon after the soldiers and even today the park's beauties are interrupted by the West Point Sewage Treatment Plant.

Discovery Park Nature Trail is a 2.8-mile loop, circling past all park entrances and intersecting the park's many side trails and beach access routes. On your blufftop tour you'll wander past Army housing, a Native American cultural center (Daybreak Star Arts Center) and intersect a couple of half-mile long side trails that lead down to the beach: South Beach Trail, North Beach Trail, West Point Trail.

The nature trail offers excellent views of Puget Sound and the distant Olympic range. Keen-eyed hikers may spot seals, sea lions and porpoises off park shores.

Begin your tour (most folks travel in a counter-clockwise direction) from the park visitor center or from the parking area at North Gate.

Access: From downtown, head north on 15th Avenue to Dravus Street. Turn west and drive a half-mile to 20th Avenue West. Turn right and enter Discovery Park. Stop at the visitor center to pick up a trails map. *By bus:* Bus service to Discovery Park includes the #19 to South Gate and the #33 to East Gate.

 Carkeek Park

Piper's Creek Trail

Just 2 miles round trip; to Richmond Beach Park is 9 miles round trip.

North Seattle's Carkeek Park is a fine assemblage of beach and bluff that offers a variety of easy walking routes. Most of the bluff paths offer superb vistas of Puget Sound and the Olympic Mountains.

Even on a day when Seattle is fog-bound and view-less, the park is well-worth a visit to see the salmon spawn. Chum salmon begin arriving in October or November and can be seen from several observation points along Piper's Creek.

The featured pathway ascends from the shoreline through a lush canyon, crisscrossing Piper's Creek several times. As the canyon narrows, choose from any of several return paths looping through the woods to the south of the canyon. Back at the bluffs high above the beach and railroad tracks, enjoy excellent bay views.

Intrepid beach-walkers can hike from Carkeek Park to Richmond Beach Park, 4.5 miles north. (If the tide's too high for safe beach-walking, hikers can retreat atop a sea wall.) A half-mile out is isolated Whiskey Cove, where smugglers landed cargo during Prohibition. The beach path passes some wild bluffs cut by creeks cascading toward shore, and continues under sometimes-visible-sometimes-not residences to Richmond Beach, former quarry site of the Richmond Beach Sand and Gravel Company.

Access: From downtown Seattle, head north on Elliott Avenue, continuing on as it becomes 15th Avenue West and takes you over the Ballard Bridge. Bearing east, the avenue becomes Holman Road North-west. Continue to Third Avenue Northwest and turn right, Turn left on Northwest 110th Street, which becomes Carkeek Park Drive and leads to two parking lots and the trailheads in Carkeek Park.

 Green Lake

Green Lake Trail
Around Green Lake is a 2.8 mile loop.

If you want to go where no one has gone before, avoid this walk; if, on the other hand, you want to go where everyone in Seattle goes, head for Green Lake. More than two million exercisers—walkers, joggers, cyclists, in-line skaters and baby stroller pushers—use Green Lake Trail, making it the most popular trail in the Pacific Northwest. Walkers account for about one-third of the trail users.

This North Seattle park's attractions are basic: lawns, plenty of trees, views of Mt. Rainier and two lake-circling paths. Green Lake is the one green scene in the Pacific Northwest where the scene overpowers the green, where people-watching is the leading form of outdoor recreation. The crowds are particularly awesome on summer Sundays when as many as 10,000 people may visit the park, and some 1,000 an hour use the paths.

While often crowded, the park is not altogether

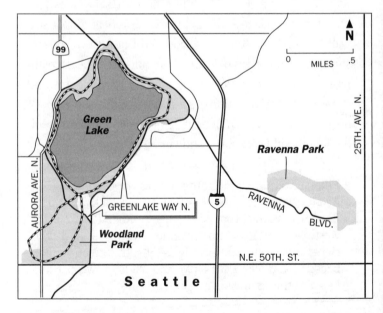

chaotic thanks to a couple of rules, the primary one being that visitors afoot must travel in a clockwise direction, those on wheels counterclockwise. The newcomer who fails to heed the method to this madness will be roundly scolded by the locals.

A quieter walk can be had at dawn, or on cold autumn and winter days. During these low-traffic times, you might be able to appreciate the beauty of little Green Lake, and count many species of resident and migratory waterfowl.

Access: From downtown Seattle, take Interstate 5 north five miles to Exit 170. Head west a half-mile on Ravenna Boulevard to a stop sign and turn right on East Green Lake Drive North. At the first stop light, turn left into Green Lake's main parking lot. If no parking is available here, park along East Green Lake Drive.

 Bainbridge Island

The Walkabout, Ft. Ward Trails
A half-dozen 1- to 2.5-mile walks.

A half-hour ferry ride across Puget Sound from metro Seattle delivers you to Bainbridge Island, an intriguing combination of forested retreat, busy marina and bedroom community.

The isle's hilly terrain does not seem to discourage cyclists, who arrive in droves. The hill-walking is pretty good, too, and much easier than the cycling.

If the weather cooperates, Seattle-Bainbridge Island ferry passengers enjoy grand views of Seattle's skyline set against the dramatic backdrop of the Cascades, as well as Over-the-rail vistas up and down Puget Sound, including the Olympic Mountains looming over the woodsy slopes of the approaching Island.

Bainbridge Island had few roads or people until the 1920s, when auto ferry service began. No doubt the frequent ferryboats have changed the character of the island from an isolated farming and shipbuilding backwater into a pricey-by-Puget Sound-standards bedroom community.

Bainbridge offered the good life for the island's first residents, too, anthropologists suggest. The Muckleshoots, Duwamish and Suquamish who lived on the island and fished offshore harvested abundant salmon and shellfish and lived in well-constructed cedar-planked dwellings.

A few woodsy suburbs aside, most of the island remains a natural environment. Greeting you at the ferry dock are gulls, kingfishers, great blue herons and many more shorebirds.

Begin your Bainbridge exploration with a stop at the Visitor Information Center located one block up from the ferry terminal at 509 Winslow Way East. Ask for the free

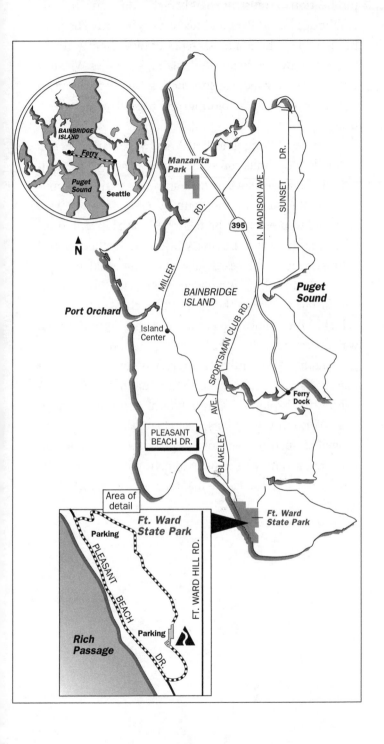

143

publication "Trails of Bainbridge" put out by the Bainbridge Island Park and Recreation District. The publication offers thumbnail sketches of nine short walks.

In the town of Bainbridge Island, known as Winslow until 1991, a good leg-stretcher is The Walkabout, a mile-long footpath exploring the Eagle Harbor waterfront.

The best hiking is in Fort Ward State Park, where a two-mile loop links forest and shore. The locale's commanding marine views made it attractive to the U.S. military at the turn of the century. Gun batteries were designed to protect the Bremerton Naval Shipyard located across the water. During World War II, the fort had submarine nets out, ready to snag enemy invaders.

Trails drop from a wooded picnic site down a fern- and fir-filled slope to the shore. A beach road (closed to vehicles) runs above the park's shoreline. From the road, walkers can join short trails leading to shore.

Another short hike (2.25 miles) can be found at Manzanita Park, situated in the middle of the island. A nature trail explores the trees typical of northwest habitats—Western yew, Sitka spruce, hemlock, white pine—as well as such related flora as huckleberry, skunk cabbage and a variety of ferns. No manzanita though; early settlers mistook the native madrone for manzanita.

 Tiger Mountain

Tradition Lake Loop, Tiger Mountain Trail

From Tradition Plateau Trailhead, hike 2.5 to 10 miles or more round trip.

If you want trails, Tiger Mountain has trails—some 60 miles worth—including hill climbs with views, short loops, long loops and 16-mile Tiger Mountain Trail, adjudged by some trail connoisseurs as one of the nation's best wild edge-of-the-metropolis footpaths. From the upper slopes of the 3,000-foot mountain, hikers savor panoramas of Mounts Rainier and St. Helens to the south, the Olympic Mountains and San Juan Islands to the west, and Pugetopolis from Tacoma to Seattle to Everett.

The wooded mountain is the centerpiece of Tiger Mountain State Forest, which came under governmental protection in 1980. Part of the mountain is managed in a wilderness-like state while another part is a "working forest" where some logging is allowed. Tiger Mountain, whose main High Point Trailhead is easily accessible from Interstate 90, offers year-round hiking and is thus a popular destination.

An easy introduction to the Tiger is via a 2.5-mile tree-lined loop around Tradition Lake. You'll have plenty of company along this popular path.

For a great view, make the five-mile round trip climb to the 2,522-foot summit of West Tiger Mountain #3. Tradition Trail is the most favored of several routes to the top. To stretch it out a bit, try a 10-mile loop around West Tiger.

Ambitious hikers will tackle Tiger Mountain Trail which travels through both the working and wilderness sides of the state forest. An ancient fir forest and terrific views make this 16-mile one-way jaunt one to remember.

Access: From Interstate 90, east of Seattle and just east of Issaqua, take the High Point exit (Exit 20). Proceed south under I-90, then turn right on the frontage road. Proceed 0.4 mile to a turnaround where a gate crosses the road. Walk 0.6 mile up the road to reach Tradition Plateau Trailhead, a pleasant place with picnic tables.

By bus: Metro Bus #21 makes a stop a bit north of the I-90 High Point Interchange.

San Juan Island National Historic Park

Interpretive, Bell Point, Mt. Young Trails
1 to 4 miles round trip.

San Juan Island National Historic Park, off the coast of Washington in the island chain of the same name, offers not only an offbeat and obscure page from American history, but some fine hiking as well. Trails lead through the forest, along wind-swept island shores, and to a couple of summits with fine views of Canadian islands and the American mainland.

The park, established in 1966, commemorates the peaceful settlement of the 19th-century Pig War, as it came to be known. Its two parcels, about 11 miles apart at opposite ends of the island, encompass the camps where opposing American and British troops were posted from 1859 to 1872.

San Juan Island is a year-round destination. While the off-season in many parts of the Pacific Northwest means "see you next summer," here it means no crowds, cool-but-not-frigid temperatures and a less expensive holiday. The San Juans are located in the "rain shadow" between the mountains of Vancouver Island and Washington's Olympic Mountains. Some island boosters claim an average of 247 sunny days a year. Nevertheless, be sure to pack rain gear and your best water-repellent walking shoes.

Most of the island's services and accommodations are in Friday Harbor, though there a handful of B&Bs and resorts in the interior and on other shores. For hiking information, be sure to stop at the National Park Service's Visitor Center, near the corner of First and Spring Streets.

Not to be missed in Friday Harbor is the superb Whale Museum. Some outstanding exhibits explain the evolution and behavior of the local orcas (killer whales).

But it was the Pig War that put San Juan Island on the map. Only one shot was fired and there was only one casualty: a pig. Yet the fallen porker created an international incident, one that brought American and Great Britain to the brink of war.

The year was 1859. For more than 40 years, Britain and the United State had been jockeying for position in the Pacific Northwest. By virtue of an 1846 treaty, possession of all lands south of the 49th Parallel in the Oregon Territory belonged to the United States. The treaty language was ambiguous, however, and both sides claimed San Juan Island.

The British supported Hudson's Bay Company, the dominant presence on San Juan, and believed the island to be part of Queen Victoria's domain. An American settler, Lyman Cutlar, had a different view, and planted a potato patch on land claimed by Hudson's Bay. When a Hudson's Bay pig repeatedly rooted around Cutlar's potatoes, he shot it.

Tempers flared. The governor of British Columbia sent a ship and the Royal Marines. Cutlar appealed to American authorities, who also sent troops. Both sides reinforced their positions—the Americans at the southeast tip of the island, the British on the northwest shore.

There followed 13 years of gridlock between diplomats but peaceful cohabitation (and many joint social activities) between the militias. Finally, the boundary question was submitted to Kaiser Wilhelm I of Germany to decide. He ruled in favor of the Americans.

Today at British Camp, you can visit a blockhouse and a couple of restored buildings from the old garrison, as well as a formal English garden, originally planted by the homesick soldiers.

British Camp offers a pair of walks. Mt. Young Trail (2.5 miles round trip, with 600-foot elevation gain) begins at the picnic area and ascends through a forest of fir and madrone to the summit, where the British main-

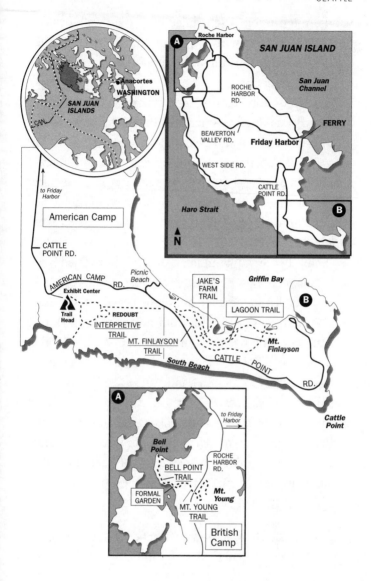

tained an observation post. The panoramic view takes in Canada's Vancouver Island and Gulf Islands, Washington's Olympic Mountains and Mt. Baker.

Bell Point Trail (one mile round trip) begins near the shoreline at the north end of camp, then meanders through the woods to Bell Cove.

American Camp has a much wilder feel than British Camp—a bold headlands lashed by fierce southerly winds. You can join a scheduled ranger-led walk or take the mile-long interpretive trail on your own. The path starts from the visitor center and loops out onto the bluffs to Pickett's Redoubt.

The redoubt (earthworks where cannons were mounted) was dug by Americans under the supervision of Lt. Henry Roberts, a 22-year-old engineer fresh out of West Point. Roberts went on to have a long and honorable military career, but it's his passion for parliamentary procedure that we remember him for. Even today he has the last word on the subject with his *Roberts' Rules of Order.*

South Beach, a two-mile expanse of shore piled high with driftwood logs, offers a superb coast walk. A couple of picnic tables are perched above the beach. At low tide, you can walk to Cattle Point (four miles round trip).

Another fine walk from American Camp is the 2.5-mile loop up Mt. Finlayson. From atop the mountain you get views of Mt. Rainier and Vancouver Island.

About halfway between British Camp and American Camp, on the west side of the island, is Lime Kiln State Park, a stretch of shore that's superb for whale-watching. Both orcas and minke whales can be seen regularly throughout the summer months as they pass the west side of the San Juan Islands.

Access: San Juan Island is reached by Washington state ferries from Anacortes, 83 miles north of Seattle.

OLYMPIC
NATIONAL PARK

CHAPTER TEN

OLYMPIC NATIONAL PARK

The tops of the enormous trees disappear into the drizzly clouds. Around me tower Sitka spruce and maple, giants cloaked, nearly choked, by thick trailing tendrils of spike moss, lichen and epiphytes, whose roots gather nourishment from the very air.

Here in the Olympic Rainforest is an uncommon alchemy of prodigious rainfall, glacier-carved river valleys, a never-felled forest of Douglas fir and red cedar cradled between the Pacific Ocean and snows that never melt, creating the awesome growing power normally associated with warmer forests.

Maybe it's the darkness of the forest primeval; maybe it's a kind of humility that comes to humans in the presence of living things that were growing here long before Europeans landed on America's shores, but I find myself walking through the forest with my head down, eyes on the ground—on the rotting logs festooned with fungus, on the forest floor carpeted with moss, on the salamander that slithers across my path.

Like most visitors, I came to see the big trees. Here in Big Trees Grove is one of the most awe-inspiring stands of Douglas fir remaining on the Olympic Peninsula. The trees: eight to 10 feet in diameter, 275-feet high, 500 or more years old.

In addition to gaping at the great trees, I wanted to get a feel for the whole forest, the only rain forest in North America. Exploring the dripping western valleys of the Olympic Peninsula was a particularly tempting adventure when contemplated from the semi-arid, drought-plagued city where I dwell. The perfect plan: spend my days walking the rainy woods along the Hoh, Quinault and Queets rivers, and my nights warm and dry in the Lake Quinault Lodge.

Up until a century or so ago, the rain forest was considered a place to avoid, not visit—Hell with a cloud cover. Long after America was crossed, conquered, and compartmentalized into states, and even after the Pacific Northwest's Manifest Destiny was made manifest, the Olympic Rainforest remained unexplored, a forest incognito, hidden in the clouds. Deepest, darkest America, like deepest, darkest Africa, was said to be a place of man-eating tigers and cannibals. In 1890, Washington governor Eugene Semple described the Olympic Rainforest: "It is a land of mystery—awe inspiring in its mighty constituents and wonder-making in its unknown expanse."

The unknown expanse baffled even the most learned scientists of the day. The many rivers meandering from the west side of the Olympics to the Pacific did not seem large enough to carry the incredible amounts of rain that fell upon the range. Surely a giant inland valley or great lake must be capturing the water; or perhaps it found its way to the sea by way of some underground chasm.

Twelve feet of rain a year is a lot of moisture. It drips from the trees, soaks the forest floor, collects in bogs, thunders over falls and cascades down gorges with such velocity that I wonder how the native salmon can possibly make it back upstream to spawn.

And of course it's the rain that continually nourishes the forests—towering stands of red cedar and Sitka spruce, Douglas fir and western hemlock. In the late afternoon gloom the forest seems to me exotic, even extra-terrestrial—all those lichens and liverworts, ferns and mosses creating a green world unlike any other.

Near day's end sharply-angled shafts of amber sunlight penetrate the treetops to create a kind of long, lingering alpenglow over the wet ultra-green world below. It's a peculiar Pacific Northwest kind of sunset: liquid sunshine that soaks into the earth.

The rain forest even makes its own rain; the tall thick canopy condenses water out of the moist air, from the very clouds, adding in some areas 30 inches to the annual rainfall.

Scientists are just beginning to learn how a rain forest canopy creates a separate climate, a microclimate, how it shelters the forest from wind and cold, moderates heat and humidity, how it filters sunlight for photosynthesis in varying amounts for different species of rain forest plants. No doubt it's difficult to study the canopy of rain forest, an ethereal ecology arching hundreds of feet above the forest floor.

Deep-blue Lake Quinault was already a popular resort area when President Theodore Roosevelt came to visit. Just one ride through the rain forest and one night at the lake prompted him to decree a portion of Olympic National Forest was off-limits to logging. Another President Roosevelt, Franklin Delano, stayed at Quinault Lodge in 1938 and became an enthusiastic supporter of a new Olympic National Park, established later that same year. Supreme Court Justice and supreme Washington state conservationist William O. Douglas was instrumental in the addition of 62 miles of coastline to Olympic National Park in the 1950s and 1960s.

Franklin Roosevelt often spoke of his great love for the Pacific Northwest and recalled that he almost came here as a young man when Weyerhauser Lumber Company offered him a job. How different world history might have been had FDR become chief executive of a timber company in Washington state instead of chief executive of a nation in Washington, D.C.!

One of Olympic National Park's glories is the close proximity of its ancient forests to its even more ancient glaciers. It's a magnificent rain forest walk to Olympus

Boardwalk trails probe the Olympic Rainforest.

Guard Station; from there, mountaineers continue to Blue Glacier, about halfway up Olympus, then climb over fields of ice and snow to the summit. Trekking through the rain forest then scaling Mt. Olympus—hikers, it doesn't get any better than this. Olympic National Park's nearly one million acres are an astounding collection of glacier-clad mountains, rain forests and the Pacific Northwest's wildest shore.

Mention rain forests and most of us think of steamy jungles, of Amazonia, Malaysia, or equatorial Africa. Such rain forests are often in the news. We read of trees clear-cut at an awesome rate with possibly disastrous effects to the ozone layer. We watch the evening news and sympathize with the plight of indigenous people displaced, endangered birds and amphibians dispossessed. We criticize the burger barons, whose fast-food franchises need mega-tons of cheap beef, available fastest and cheapest from the rain forest, which is cut and cleared, quick-seeded with grass, and soon transformed into a quickie cattle operation run by local capitalist cowboys, all to support our insatiable hamburger habit. Meanwhile, a conservative radio talk show host from New York declares: "It's not a rain forest, it's a jungle," rallying his anti-eco audience by identifying the forest with snakes and slime, not baby lemurs and biodiversity.

As endangered as they are, tropical rain forests are many. Temperate rain forests, however, are very few: in Patagonia, New Zealand, Australia, and on the Olympic Peninsula of Washington and Vancouver Island.

The Olympic Rainforest is protected from further predation by timber companies and government bureaucrats by its national park status, wilderness designation, and by its status as a United Nations World Heritage Site, joining Hawaii's volcanoes and the great pyramids of Egypt as places worth saving for the future generations that will live on this ever-more-crowded planet.

The Olympic Mountains, their classic snowcone peaks spiked with evergreens, their glaciers and alpine lakes, make for a captivating photo. The Olympic Rainforest, however, offers no such photo opportunity: much too much green, much too dark, and everything intertwined with everything else.

When he spoke of the rain forest, John Muir observed, "Nature was trying to see how many of her darlings she can get together in one mountain wreath."

Memories, however imperfect, are all you can take from the rain forest.

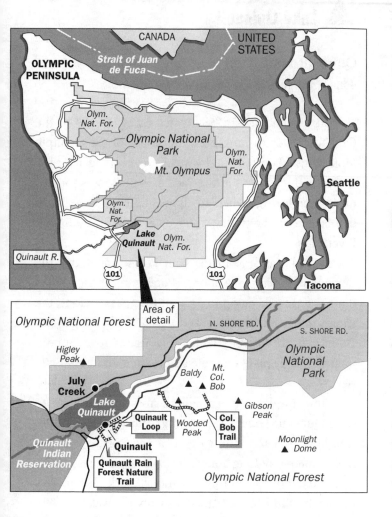

CANADA

UNITED STATES

OLYMPIC PENINSULA

Strait of Juan de Fuca

Olym. Nat. For.

Olympic National Park

Mt. Olympus

Olym. Nat. For.

Seattle

Olym. Nat. For.

Lake Quinault

Olym. Nat. For.

Quinault R.

101

101

Tacoma

Area of detail

Olympic National Forest

N. SHORE RD.

S. SHORE RD.

Olympic National Park

Higley Peak ▲

July Creek ●

Baldy ▲

Mt. Col. Bob ▲

Lake Quinault

Quinault Loop

Wooded Peak ▲

Col. Bob Trail

Gibson Peak ▲

Quinault

Moonlight ▲ Dome

Quinault Indian Reservation

Quinault Rain Forest Nature Trail

Olympic National Forest

 Lake Quinault

Quinault Loop Trail

4 mile loop through Quinault Rain Forest.

Lake Quinault is a beauty, fed by two forks of the Quinault River rushing from the slopes of the Olympic Mountains. Located midway between its glacier-fed source and its mouth at the Pacific, the lake was formed during the Ice Age when an alpine glacier shoveled rock debris across the valley, thus damming the Quinault River.

The lake and Quinault Rain Forest are under the domain of Olympic National Forest, an agency that's done a great job designing a trail that passes along the shores of Lake Quinault and meanders among giant Douglas fir in the aptly named Big Trees Grove. Superb interpretive displays en route add to the rain forest experience.

From the lakeshore, walkers cross a wide lawn to Lake Quinault Lodge, a sprawling, cedar-shingled structure built in 1920. The lodge is a great place to spend nights after day-long forays into the rain forest. It's a grand old hotel, befitting a national park that always makes the short list of "America's Crown Jewels."

The comfortable lobby is the place to mingle. Beams and window trim are etched with Indian motifs. Guests read and talk quietly around a great hearth, address postcards at writing desks, relax in the Grandma-style sofas and wicker chairs.

Quinault Rain Forest Nature Trail is a half-mile loop that climbs through Big Trees Grove, one of the most awe-inspiring stands of Douglas fir remaining on the Olympic Peninsula. The eight-foot diameter, 275-foot high giants began growing about the time Columbus set sail for the New World.

Landmark Lake Quinault Lodge.

Quinault Loop Trail is a four-mile loop that begins near the lodge and U.S. Forest Service ranger station. The trail meanders along the lakeshore past tangles of blackberry and salmonberry bushes, then crosses South Shore Road and explores the rain forest. Maidenhair and sword ferns line the path, which passes beneath towering fir, spruce and cedar. Part of the trail is an elevated wooden boardwalk that crosses a mucky, spooky-looking bog.

Six miles from U.S. 101 on South Shore Road is an entry point to 12,000-acre Colonel Bob Wilderness, set aside in 1984. Colonel Bob Trail ascends 7.25 steep miles up fir- and cedar-forested slopes, past meadows known for spectacular summer wildflowers, to the summit of Colonel Bob Peak (4,492 feet). Grand clear-day vistas of Quinault country, as well as the snowy peaks of the Olympic range, including Mt. Olympus, are the hiker's reward for reaching this peak.

Access: From Highway 101, some 43 miles north of Hoquiam, turn east on South Shore Road and follow it 1.5 miles to the trailhead parking lot on the south side of the road. You can also pick up this trail at Lake Quinault Lodge, as well as Willaby and Falls Creek campgrounds. At yet another trailhead—the U.S. Forest Service's Quinault Ranger Station—you can get the latest trail information and maps.

 Enchanted Valley

East Fork, Quinault River

From Graves Creek Campground to Enchanted Valley is 13.1 miles one way; to O'Neil Creek Camp is 6.6 miles one way.

The treetops drip-drip-drip as you walk through the mist along the East Fork of the Quinault River. The trail leads through a grand forest of giant Douglas fir and cedar, entwined with thickets of vine maple, devils club and huckleberry. Peeping out from among the ferns are Queencup beadlilies and bunchberry dogwood.

Halfway to Enchanted Valley the forest opens up just enough to peer up-river at the glaciated peaks. For good reason, Enchanted Valley was a favorite of the late Supreme Court justice and great conservationist William O. Douglas. The Washington native quietly lobbied the executive and legislative branches of government in that other Washington on the Potomac to help preserve the rain forest.

The river is spanned by a suspension bridge in Enchanted Valley. Dozens of cascades trickle and crash down the walls of this dramatic, glacier-sculpted valley. Farther up the valley, the Quinault River spills into a multitude of braided channels. Enchanted Valley Chalet, a two-story log ranger station.

If you're backpacking you'll want to linger in one of the valley's many good campsites. Otherwise, you plunge back into the rain forest to return to Quinault by nightfall.

The river, pale green in the morning, is sometimes a frothy, snowmelt-swollen, milky white in mid-afternoon. Below its headwaters the Quinault is a wild thing, an altogether different river from the one that fills Quinault Lake, then meanders peacefully to the Pacific.

Access: From Highway 101, turn east on Lake Quinault's South Shore Road and drive 19 miles to the trailhead and Graves Creek Campground and Ranger Station.

 Queets River

Queets River Trail

To Spruce Bottom Camp is 10 miles round trip; to Harlow Bottom is 14 miles round trip.

To join Queets River Trail you first have to cross the Queets River. And that's not easy. Not only is the Queets River one of the largest rivers on the Olympic Peninsula, it's probably the coldest—swollen with meltwater from glaciers atop Mt. Queets and Mt. Olympus.

Rangers are quite correct in warning that the crossing is safe only in late summer or early autumn (after snowmelt, before fall rains). Hikers make the crossing with sturdy stick and great care. Sometimes rangers suggest crossing the nearby Sams River and then the Queets; check with them.

Your reward for crossing the Queets is access to the most isolated of the Olympic rain forests. The crossing at the start of Queets River Trail discourages most walkers, and even though the Queets is famous as a steelhead stream, few fishermen chance the crossing to reach the grand angling up-river.

The excellent trail (probably in good shape because it is so little used) is actually an ancient pathway used by the native Quinault to hunt elk. It follows the river bottomland, soon plunging into spruce-hemlock rain forest garlanded with mosses. At 2.5 miles from the trailhead, a short side trail leads to the base of one of the world's largest Douglas firs.

Five miles of hiking through the forest brings you to Spruce Bottom Camp. The drip-drip-drip of the rain forest alternates with the mesmerizing roar of the Queets as the path meanders among grotesque big-leaf maple festooned with spike-moss. Turnaround point for a long day hike is Harlow Bottom, home to some huge Sitka spruce, a species that grows much higher here than its cousins in Alaska.

The late naturalist Roger Tory Peterson once calculated that the Olympic Rainforest is weighted down with more living matter than any other place on earth. I don't know how he made his calculation but I find no reason to doubt it here along the Queets River. Truly it is hard to imagine a greener world than this one.

 Hoh Rain Forest

Hoh Trail

From Rain Forest Visitors Center to Happy Four Camp is 11.5 miles round trip with200-foot elevation gain; to Olympus Ranger Station is 18 miles round trip.

The Hoh River area is the only part of the rain forest where the National Park Service has a public presence: a small visitors center, an interpreted nature trail that leads through the positively Gothic Hall of Mosses, and friendly rangers who greet the curious refugees from Highway 101 and the serious mountaineer bound for Mt. Olympus.

The Hoh Rainforest is all the more amazing to people because of what they've driven through to get here: clear-cuts right up to the park boundary. Then Hoh!

Along the Hoh Trail is a marvelous rain forest: ferns taller than the tallest hiker, hemlocks wider than the rooms at the Lake Quinault Lodge. Fallen logs are upholstered with moss, the ground is carpeted with it. Above the lush understory rise huge fir, cedar and spruce, their great trunks rising without limbs 100 feet or more, like classic Doric columns.

But unlike columns, each tree, especially the older ones, is unique. An old-growth tree is a survivor, a rugged individualist with thick folded skin, twisted limbs and a broken crown.

Best day hike is the 5.75-mile jaunt up the Hoh River to Happy Four Camp. Three more miles of rambling brings you to Olympus Guard Station, perched between the ancient forest and even more ancient glaciers on Mt. Olympus. From here, mountaineers continue to Blue Glacier, about halfway up Olympus, then climb over fields of ice and snow to the summit.

Access: From Highway 101 in the town of Forks, head south 12 miles. Turn east on Hoh River Road and proceed 19 miles to road's end and the trailhead at Rain Forest Visitors Center.

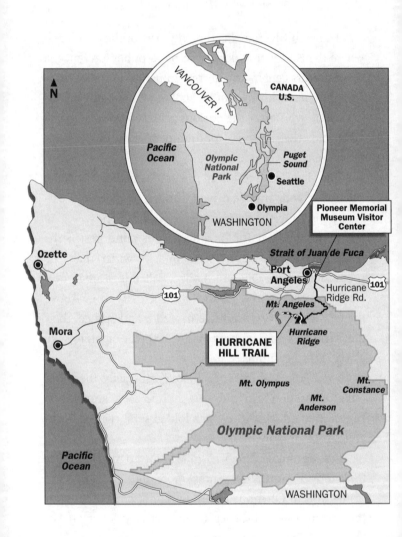

 Hurricane Ridge

Hurricane Hill Trail

To Hurricane Ridge is 3 miles round trip with 800-foot elevation gain; longer hikes possible.

Mile-high Hurricane Ridge, perched on the northern edge of the Olympic Range, offers postcard panoramas of Olympic National Park, as well as the Strait of Juan de Fuca and Vancouver Island.

Road access to the national park from the north side is limited to just two roads, one of which—Hurricane Ridge Road—is a scenic gem. The wide road begins at Port Angeles and winds around Mt. Angeles, offering excellent vistas as it climbs to Hurricane Ridge.

Far-sighted park administrators closed the last mile and a half of the road to auto traffic in the late 1950s and converted it to a footpath, thus offering an easy, but inspiring, hike for visitors driving up Hurricane Ridge.

The hiking season for Hurricane Ridge is short—late June through September. Naturalist programs are held daily from July 1 to Labor Day. Wildflower season is about the same as the hiking season: Look for avalanche lilies, lupine and wallflowers in June and July; blue bells of Scotland, larkspur and Olympic aster in July and August.

Signed Hurricane Hill Trail ascends through meadowland and occasional clusters of subalpine fir. You'll spot some delightful picnic spots at the top of the 5,757-foot hill.

Up top, unfold your park map and look for Mt. Anderson far to the southeast, as well as many more mighty snow-capped Olympic peaks. To the east are The Needles, well-named you'll agree. Just down below, 10 miles to the north, is Port Angeles; 20 miles farther, across the Strait of Juan de Fuca, is Victoria. In the misty blue distance, the San Juan Islands float upon the north-east horizon, and beyond them loom Mt. Baker and the awesome Cascades.

Besides the jaunt up Hurricane Hill, other easy family outings nearby include Big Meadow Trail, which begins at the Hurricane Ridge Visitor Center. Three inter-connecting paved paths explore a grassy, wildflower-dotted alpine meadow. Along this trail grow tiny wind-bowed fir trees, grown to a height of only two feet because of the inclement weather and other environmental factors.

An 8.5-mile round trip ascent to the shoulder of scenic 6,454-foot Mt. Angeles begins from a trailhead at the Hurricane Ridge parking area.

First stop for park visitors and prospective Hurricane Ridge hikers should be Olympic National Park's Visitor Center on Hurricane Ridge Road on the outskirts of Port Angeles. Exhibits highlight the park's flora and fauna, and the well-informed park staff can provide updates about road and trail conditions.

Access: From Highway 101 in Port Angeles, drive 17 miles up Hurricane Ridge Road to road's end at the Hurricane Ridge parking area.

Olympic National Park Coast

Coast Trail

62 miles one way.

It's Washington's wettest and wildest shore, a 62-mile long strip practically unchanged since famed explorer Captain James Cook sailed by in 1778. Monumental sea stacks, dramatic capes and coves, rocks and reefs— Olympic National Park's ocean shore is one to remember.

All is not quiet on the western front of Olympic National Park, especially in winter when huge waves, high winds and heavy rains lash the shore. The surf tosses giant logs upon the shore like so many matchsticks. Ah, but Pacific Northwesterners sometimes make a spectator sport of it: "Winter storm watching," they call it. And between storms the hiking is magnificent—the wildest shore on the continental U.S.

This land on the far northwestern part of the continental U.S. is pounded by rain; some 100 inches a year falls on these beaches in the shadow of mighty Mt. Olympus. Of course the weather is worse inland: the adjacent rain forest is rainier, and 7,965-foot Mt. Olympus gathers 200 inches of annual precipitation— mostly in the form of snow.

Three-fourths of the coast's prodigious rainfall soaks the shore during the late fall-winter-early spring rainy season. However, even the summer hiking season averages a few inches a month.

When storms are brewing, land and sea and sky each assume a different color of darkness, gun-metal gray, the color of stone and the color of ash, silver and slate, livid and leaden.

Above the shore inland thrives a forest of Sitka spruce, red cedar and hemlock, towering above a forest floor that's a tangle of ferns, mosses, salal, sorrel and ocean spray. Elk, raccoons, black-tailed deer and black bear roam the bluffs above the beach.

Double-crested cormorants, black oystercatchers, gulls and great blue herons are among the frequently seen airborne denizens of land's end. Sea stacks (the tall off-shore rocks) are mini-wildlife refuges, offering sanctuary for murres, guillemots, auklets and puffins, the favorite sighting of every binocular-equipped child.

Minus tides present opportunities for exploration of this coast's abundant tidepools, teeming with mussels, starfish, anemones, sea urchins, rock oysters, hermit crabs and many more creatures.

Certainly this coast is a wilderness by all outward appearances—charcoal-gray beaches heaped with humongous driftwood logs, spruce-spiked headlands enshrouded in the mist. It's managed as a wilderness by the National Park Service. Within this public domain, and adding to it's end-of-the-world feeling, are three American Indian holdings: the Ozette Reservation on the north side of Cape Alava, the Quileute Reservation at La Push and the Hoh Reservation on the south side of the Hoh River.

Although the main body of Olympic National Park was created in 1938, it wasn't until much later that the coastal strip was preserved. In 1958, Supreme Court Justice William O. Douglas led a group of conservation-ists on a hike to call public attention to this then-endan-gered shore.

The hiking opportunities are many: weekend and week-long backpacking trips, half-day and all-day treks, easy beach walks and—with the possible exception of California's Lost Coast—the most difficult shoreline treks in America.

Backpacking is the only way to see two 17-mile long sections of this coast, which have no road access.

The beaches themselves are of two varieties: long, wide sand strands and minor coves bounded on each end by rocky points. Some of these rocky points can only be rounded at low tide. Others must be surmounted by forest trails that climb inland before returning the hiker to the beach.

Olympic National Park beaches are open all year, but you may have to brave the rain or attempt to time your visit between storms. Temperatures are relatively mild for this part of the world—rarely dropping below freezing or above 65 degrees F. Summer, the most popular hiking season, is often cool, moist and foggy.

For some hikers, autumn is the favorite time for beachcombing. Thanksgiving weekend is a particularly popular time for family adventures here, although the weather is often at its worst.

Although some intrepid backpackers do hike the whole 62-mile length of coast, most hikers favor one-, two- and three-day journeys. The complete absence of local public transportation means that overnighters must make car shuttle arrangements or plan round trip hikes.

The easiest length of ocean beach to explore is the southern quarter which is paralleled for a dozen miles by U.S. Highway 101. (Unlike its Oregon and California cousins, Washington's Highway 101 doesn't touch the Pacific shore in many places.)

Kalaloch (pronounced Kuh-lay-lock), a picturesque lodge with cabins and a restaurant, is an ideal base for exploring this southern coast. The lodge overlooks Kalaloch Creek and a long, sandy beach that attracts surf fishermen, clammers and hikers.

Just north of the lodge is Kalaloch Campground. The park's most popular campground is filled nearly every night during the summer months, and on many weekends as well. Kalaloch Information Station, located on the east side of the highway, has maps, as well as the latest tide, weather and hiking information.

Within six miles of Kalaloch are seven beaches, all easily accessible from Highway 101. You can roam from one beach to the other, but make sure you consult a tide table and time your walk for low tide.

The 17-mile hike from Third Beach to the Hoh River is almost as rugged as its northern counterparts. Sometimes the long sand ladders at Taylor Point intimidate backpackers, sometimes the isolation of this coast and the slow progress across the sand are simply disheartening to the hiker accustomed to thinking of beach hikes as a lark. Carry a tide table and don't be surprised if it takes you three days to finish this hike.

The hike from Sand Point south to Rialto Beach is another memorable 17-miler. En route, the hiker passes several memorials to ships that were wrecked upon this shore. Obstacles along the way include difficult-to-get-around headlands, lots of rock-hopping, and miles of wet sand.

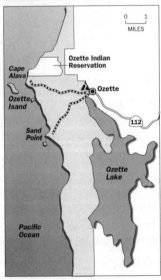

Cape Alava, Sand Point

Cape Alava, Sand Point Trails

9.3 miles round trip.

In the Lake Ozette area a triangle loop trail offers a sampling of the national park's stunning coastline. Plank boardwalks form two sides of the triangle, three miles of wilderness beach the other.

Native people have lived on this coast for centuries. A village site at Cape Alava, buried by a mud slide some 500 years ago, preserved a multitude of artifacts that helped archeologists understand the culture and lives of these early people.

Follow the path 0.25 mile to a junction. Sand Point Trail (your return route) forks left but you bear right on Cape Alava Trail and follow the boardwalk path through a lowland forest thick with salal, huckleberry and ferns. About halfway along, you'll reach a boggy area known as Ahlstrom's Meadow. Lake Ozette pioneer Lars Ahlstrom, a native of Sweden, resided here from 1902 to 1958.

The boardwalk returns to the forest before dropping to the driftwood-strewn beach facing Ozette Island. Cape Alava and Cannonball Island are to the north.

This hike heads south a mile along the beach, reaching a minor headland called Wedding Rock. Two more miles of beach travel brings you to the misnamed Sand Point, a rocky point crowned with grass. Join a second boardwalk trail, traveling past a stand of Sitka spruce and through the lush green forest back to the trailhead.

Access: From Highway 101, five miles west of Port Angeles, turn onto Highway 112 and follow it 32 miles west to Ozette Hoko Road, just past the hamlet of Seiku. Turn south on Ozette Hoko Road and proceed 20 miles to road's end at the Ozette Ranger Station. From the parking lot, walk to the ranger station and inquire about the latest tide and trail information. The trail begins at a nearby information kiosk.

Mt. Rainier, king of the Cascades.

MT. RAINIER
NATIONAL PARK

CHAPTER ELEVEN

MT. RAINIER NATIONAL PARK

Mt. Rainier has the kind of superlatives expected of a national park: the tallest volcanic mountain in the continental U.S. (14,411 feet) and the mountain with the most active glaciers (27). Add 382 lakes and some of the finest alpine meadows in the world and you have quite a park.

Ah, but how can one judge people by their tailors' measurements or mountains by their numbers? Mt. Rainier is not merely high, it's commanding, a symmetrical beauty rising abruptly from forested lowlands. It's a snowy backdrop for Seattle, a peak presiding over lesser Cascades, an Arctic-like island floating in the clouds above a temperate zone.

During the 1950s and 1960s Mt. Rainier was always included near the top of the list of "America's crown jewels" and today makes many a "Top Ten National Parks" list. Such lists are silly of course, but they do point to respect (bordering on reverence in some instances) that visitors have for the great mountain.

The park, boasting more than 300 miles of trail, is very much oriented to hikers. Trail savvy staff answer questions and provide hiking information at a number of ranger stations and visitor centers, as well as two special Hiker Information Centers located at Longmire and White River. Rainier's pathways are as varied as you might expect of a national park that ranges from 2,000 to 14,000 feet in elevation. The park includes both short and day-long excursions for hikers of all abilities.

Chief among the pathways is the 93-mile Mt. Rainier-encircling Wonderland Trail, often regarded as the Pacific Northwest's best long-distance trail. Backpacking options are many; the park's backcountry trail camps and shelters can accommodate more than 1,000 hikers and climbers.

Paradise is the major trailhead for climbers bound for Mt. Rainier's 14,411-foot summit. For hardy, experienced hikers, a summit attempt is apt to be one to remember. It's always a serious—and sometimes a dangerous—climb requiring the use of ice axes and crampons and requiring snow and ice travel skills.

The best way to go for the serious hiker (but relatively inexperienced mountaineer) is to utilize the guide service, Rainier Mountaineers Inc. located at the Paradise trailhead. Seasoned guides offer a three-day course, including a day of practice and a two-day climb. The company will rent you the necessary equipment.

The climb begins with a trek from Paradise to a base camp at Camp Muir. Next morning you make an early morning try for the summit, then descend to Paradise. Fewer than half the six to eight thousand climbers attempting the peak per year, reach the summit.

Some 97 percent of the park's 235,612 acres were declared wilderness in 1988. With the exception of some roads, camps and concessions, most of the mountain is managed with the National Park Service's strictest conservation policies and regulations.

Four entrances—one in each corner of the square-ish park, access Mt. Rainier. The main entrance and the only one open all year is Longmire, the park's oldest developed area. James Longmire established Mineral Springs Resort here in 1884 and after Mt. Rainier became a national park in 1899, Longmire's settlement became park headquarters. Longmire's hiking trails are usually snow-free earlier in the summer than those higher on the mountain.

The other all-year visitor area is Paradise, whose hikes offer up-close views of glaciers and meadows with majestic wildflower displays. A lodge, a visitor center and a popular network of trails add to Paradise's allure.

Mt. Ranier's winters are characterized by massive snowfall. During the winter of 1971-72, a record 93.5 feet of snow fell on Paradise Ranger Station. Not until late June or July does the snowline recede up Mt. Rainier's slopes to uncover its trail network.

So high and mighty is Mt. Rainier, it's said to generate its own weather. The mountain's summit is often capped by a swirling, lens-shaped cloud formation known as a lenticular cloud, evidence of Rainier's disruption of prevailing wind patterns. Mt. Rainier and smaller Cascade peaks force moisture-laden marine air flows to drop precipitation on the western slopes. The mountain range forms a wall between Washington's wet western side and its much drier, rain shadow-situated east side.

When it's not snowing on Mt. Rainier, it's often raining, sometimes even during the supposedly dry months of July and August. "Mt. Rainiest" is the glum pun offered by those locals and visitors not enamored of a walk in the rain. While few hikers relish tramping the park's pathways in a hard rain, those who like their trails tranquil will savor a hike when the weather is foggy or misty. Instead of striving for the perfect postcard view of the snowy mountaintop, you'll notice smaller things—mosses, wildflowers, birds, chipmunks and chickadees.

Thick, old-growth forest of Douglas fir, western hemlock and western red cedar blanket the park's lower slopes below 4,000 feet. Higher up the mountain, in the 4-6,000 foot range, grow whitebark pine, subalpine fir, Alaska cedar and mountain hemlock. The trees thin out, grow shorter and more stunted with increasing elevation.

Mt. Rainier's meadows burst forth with wildflowers in awesome summer splendor. Indian paintbrush, penstemon, columbine, avalanche lily, golden rod, larkspur, western anemone, aster and buttercup are among the more than six-dozen species.

The meadows, more than any other part of the mountain, really feel the effects of Mt. Rainier's two million-plus visitors a year. A century ago, Paradise Meadows greeted just hundreds of visitors a year; now it receives hundreds of thousands. The National Park Service has implemented an ambitious plan to repair human damage—caused mainly by people wandering off main trails and blazing new ones. For the most part, the meadows will restore themselves if left alone, and hikers stay on established trails.

Along with challenges to serious mountaineers, the national park offers trails the whole family can enjoy.

 Around Mt. Rainier

Wonderland Trail

93-mile loop around Mt. Rainier

In the pantheon of long-distance pathways, Wonderland Trail occupies an exalted place. Many experienced backpackers call it the Pacific Northwest's greatest hike.

It's an old trail as national park trails go, constructed at the turn of the century just after Mt. Rainier National Park was established. Long before the park was ringed by paved highways, rangers used the Wonderland Trail to patrol Rainier on horseback. During the 1930s Civilian Conservation Corps' efforts made the trail into the nationally recognized recreation trail it is today.

Long ago, "Wonderland" was a park promoter's phrase; in this instance, the name did not overstate the region's allure. Wonderland Trail tours a grand assemblage of alpine meadows, thick forests, awesome glaciers, dramatic creeks and rivers. With every turn there is a different view up at the many faces of Mt. Rainier.

The prudent hiker will allow 10 to 14 days for a full circumnavigation of the mountain, but encounters with bad weather can considerably slow progress. In decent conditions, an average of 7 to 10 miles a day is about it, veteran hikers advise, as the trail has lots of ups and downs. Several hiking days climb 3,500 feet or so; the whole route requires gains in excess of 20,000 feet.

Some hikers figure hiking the Wonderland is a terrific summer vacation and complete the whole mountain-encircling route at one time. Others tramp the trail in sections, savoring the Wonderland a few days at a time.

Logistics are a bit complicated. Wonderland Trail camps number 18, they're situated three to seven miles apart, and reservations are required. National Park

Service policy has been to limit the number and capacity of campsites. Critics say this unduly limits backpacking, while other praise the policy and suggest it provides a superior wilderness experience for both day hikers and backpackers.

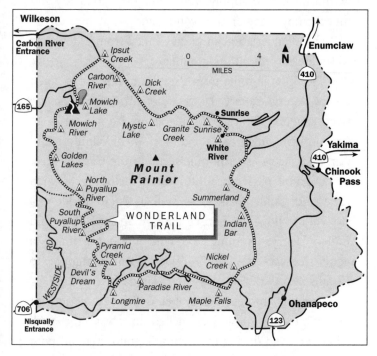

Required backcountry permits are issued at the Hiker Information Centers in Longmire and White River. As part of the permit process, you must commit to a particular trailside camp; exercise a little flexibility here because your first choice might be full.

Other camping options for experienced hikers are "cross country zones," where backpackers find their own places to camp. Such camps are required to be located at least a quarter-mile from roads and trails, and a minimum of 100 feet from any water source.

You certainly won't want to carry two weeks, or even 10 day's, worth of food on your Wonderland walk. Take advantage of the National Park Service's Food Cache Program and store a food cache or two or three. The park has detailed instruction for the right waterproof and rodent-proof containers, how to ship them (UPS) and the five stations—Paradise, Sunrise, White River, Ohana-pecosh and Longmire—where you may stash your cache. By all means try to convince friends or family to meet you with a fresh food supply; you'll enjoy the company and they'll enjoy a day on the Wonderland.

The Wonderland can be day hiked from a dozen or so trailheads around the mountain.

The 30-mile route from Paradise to Sunrise is noted for its watery scenery: lakes, waterfalls and a dramatic river canyon. On the 16-mile jaunt from Sunrise to Carbon River, hikers get up-close views of Winthrop and Carbon glaciers. The 39-mile section from Carbon River to Longmire passes beautiful lakes, including Mowich Lake and Golden Lakes, as well as such wildflower-strewn meadows as Sunset Park, Klapatche Park and Indian Henry's Hunting Grounds. A last 6.5 miles (a good one-way day hike) travels from Longmire to Paradise via Carter, Madcap and Narada falls.

Mid-July through September is the best period for hiking, as the snow has melted to reveal the trail. However, even during these months, rain, fog and poor visibility are often problems, and map and compass navigation may be required. Even during the 10-week "safe travel" window, no one will laugh at you if you carry an ice ax.

Write or call for the following park brochures: Wilderness Trip Planner, Wonderland Trail, Food Cache Planner.

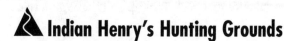 Indian Henry's Hunting Grounds

Kautz Creek Trail

To Indian Henry's Hunting Grounds is 11.5 miles round trip with 3,200-foot elevation gain.

One of the many wonders reached by Wonderland Trail and by Kautz Creek Trail is Indian Henry's Hunting Grounds, a broad, wildflower-strewn meadow.

The place names along the trail offer an interesting glimpse into Mt. Rainier climbing history. Kautz Creek Trail is named for early climber Lt. August Kautz; Indian Henry was a native Klickitat who guided late 19th-century climbers; Mt. Ararat was the hallucination of an explorer who believed Noah's Ark landed on Rainier's shoulder rather than on that other Ararat in eastern Turkey.

Part of Kautz Creek Trail is entrenched in a giant mudflat, the product of flooding from Kautz Glacier in 1947, which actually makes pretty good walking. Periodic flooding has damaged West Side Road and wiped out Tahoma Creek Trail, once the shortest route to Indian Henry's.

Beyond the mudflat, the path switchbacks through forest, nears Mt. Ararat, then continues to Indian Henry's Hunting Grounds. From this memorable meadow, many hikers opt for the 0.75-mile trip up the trail to Mirror Lake. Here photographers, amateurs and professional, attempt to capture Mt. Rainier's reflection in the lake—an image that graced many a postcard.

Indian Henry's can also be reached from Longmire via the Wonderland Trail, which climbs to a junction with Rampart Ridge Trail, then continues to Devil's Dream Camp, five miles out. A knee-jarring staircase trail (designed to combat erosion on this steep slope) takes you to Indian Henry's. With a bit of creative car shuttling, you could take Kautz Creek Trail up and the Wonderland Trail down (or vice-versa).

Access: From Mt. Rainier National Park's Nisqually Entrance Station, continue three more miles on Highway 706 to the Kautz Creek Trailhead.

Mt. Rainier—a photographer's delight from almost any angle.

Comet Falls and Van Trump Park

Comet Falls Trail

To Comet Falls is 3.8 miles round trip with 900-foot elevation gain; to Van Trump Park is 5.8 miles round trip with 1,500-foot elevation gain.

The allure of one of the park's highest waterfalls, as well as alpine views extending from nearby glaciers to distant Mount St. Helens attracts many hikers to this easy-to-access trail near Longmire. Comet Falls, a 320-foot cascade said to resemble the trail of a comet, is a beauty.

Wildlife-watching is often good in the Van Trump Park area. Pikas and marmots scamper over the rocks and even the usually elusive mountain goats are often glimpsed early in the hiking season.

Plan to get an early start on this trail. It's a popular path and trailhead parking is limited.

The path begins with a steep half-mile ascent and passes some lovely little cascades along Van Trump Creek. About 1.5 miles out, you'll get a view of Comet Falls. Enjoy viewing the falls from a couple spots on and below the trail, then tackle a mile of switchbacks to reach wildflower-dotted Van Trump Park. If Van Trump Creek isn't too high, cross it and climb north a mile to Mildred Point for a grand view of Kautz Glacier.

From Van Trump Park, you could hike to Longmire via Rampart Ridge Trail if you've arranged a car shuttle.

Access: From the national park's Nisuqally entrance drive 10 miles (four miles east of Longmire) to trailhead parking on the left side of the road. Alas, if the parking lot is filled, you'll need to choose another hike; no alternative parking is nearby.

 Paradise Meadows

Skyline Trail

From Paradise Ranger Station to Panorama Point is a 5.8-mile loop with 1,400-foot elevation gain; to Camp Muir is 9 miles round trip with 4,600-foot elevation gain.

Paradise it is in late July and August when the snow finally melts and wildflowers—glacier lilies, shooting stars, paintbrush, western anemones, Lewis monkey-flower and many more—color the slopes.

At other times of the year, Paradise means prodigious snowfall. Rainier's south slope averages 630 inches per winter and during the great winter of 1971-72, 1,122 inches, or 93.5 feet, buried the Paradise area.

Paradise, which has a large visitor center with inter-pretive exhibits, attracts both casual hikers out to see the wildflower displays and serious climbers bound for Rainier's summit. (Don't even think about picking flow-ers; it's against park regulations as is off-trail hiking in the meadows area.)

Paradise has quite a network of trails that meander the colorful meadows above the visitor center. Nisqually Vista Trail is a fairly flat one-miler, leads west through meadows to an overlook of Nisqually Glacier. A couple of short paths climb to Alta Vista, a forested promontory perched above Paradise Ranger Station.

Skyline Trail is a glorious loop through Paradise Meadows up to Panorama Point, where the hiker comes face to face with Rainier and can then turn south an see all the way to Mount St. Helens.

The preferred travel direction is clockwise, passing Nisqually Vista Trail and climbing 2.5 miles to a junction with the pathway to Camp Muir. This brutal route, used by summit-bound climbers is for top hikers only, experi-enced in snow and ice travel. Camp Muir, which includes both campsites and stone/concrete shelters is usually occupied by climbers readying for an early-morning summit assault.

Past the Camp Muir turnoff, Skyline Trail soon reaches Panorama Point, serves up terrific vistas, then heads southward and downward. For an enjoyable extension to your walk, leave the Skyline Loop by joining the path heading for Manzama Ridge, then return to Paradise via the Lakes Trail; this option adds 2.5 miles to your walk.

Access: From Highway 706 at Mt. Rainier's Nisqually Entrance Station, drive 20 miles to the upper parking lot near Paradise Ranger Station. Locate the trailhead by the restroom on the left side of the ranger station.

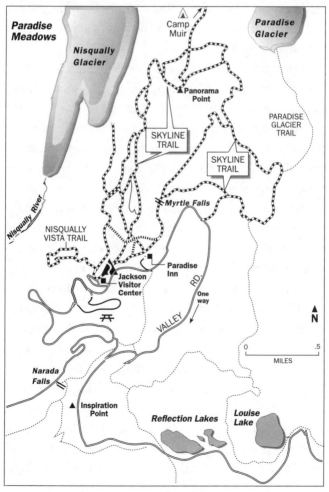

 Sunrise

To Berkeley Park is 5 miles round trip; to Grand Park is 13.5 miles round trip with 1,800-foot elevation gain.

Sunrise (elevation 6,400 feet), the highest auto-accessible point in the national park, offers stunning views of nearby glaciers and distant Cascade peaks such as Mt. Baker and Mt. Hood. A fine trail network stitches together lakes, glacier overlooks and wildflower-strewn meadows known as "parks."

Grand Park (no overstatement here) is a wide meadow perched atop a lava flow. Some say its Rainier's prettiest meadow. The volcanic soil nurtures flowering meadows that differ from others in the park such as those in the Paradise area.

Interpretive exhibits at the rustic Sunrise Visitor Center help explain the ecology and geology of Sunrise, a unique area fashioned by fire and ice.

Sunrise has a short hiking season. Not until July does the snow melt sufficiently for park crews to plow Sunrise Road. Fortifying hikers for the trail, the Sunrise Lodge cafeteria serves fast meals and snacks.

Several short trails explore Sunrise, including half-mile long Emmons Vista Trail which offers great views of Emmons Glacier. It's also a good place to plant your tripod for taking classic photos of Mt. Rainier.

Sunrise Trails also ascend panorama-providing peak-lets. Dege Peak, a 4-mile round trip jaunt on Sourdough Ridge Trail delivers vistas of the Cascades, Olympics, and even Seattle. Burroughs Mountain, a 5.5-mile round trip, also offers commanding views of Cascadia and Pugetopolis (the latter sometimes appearing as a brown smudge in the white distance).

From Sunrise, walk the 1.5 miles to little Frozen Lake, then ascend the wildflower-dotted meadows of Berkeley Park. The path dips to a waterfall on Lodi Creek then climbs to Grand Park. Meander this wide fairly flat meadow before heading back to Sunrise. Take advantage of the numerous optional trails on your return.

Access: From the park's White River entrance, follow Sunrise Road 17 miles west to the parking lot and visitor center at road's end. The Sunrise Road often does not open until early July.

Some 350 miles of lonely trail explore one of America's least-visited national parks.

NORTH CASCADES
NATIONAL PARK

CHAPTER TWELVE

NORTH CASCADES NATIONAL PARK

Sometimes it seems North Cascades National Park has more glaciers than visitors.

OK, so I'm exaggerating a little. But the park, home to 300 glaciers (half the total number in the continental U.S.) attracts only about 40,000 visitors a year. Compare this number with the nearly two million a year who flock to Mt. Rainier and then ponder that some officials consider any park with fewer than 500,000 visits to be "lightly visited."

Many park peaks, obviously named by tell-it-like-it-is early explorers and climbers, not latter-day visitor bureaus, do not, in truth, entice visitors: Damnation Peak, Desolation Peak, Forbidden Peak, and Mt. Terror.

It's certainly not for lack of scenery that people stay away from North Cascades National Park in droves. The park is a collection of snowcapped "American Alps," deep valleys, alpine lakes and thick forests.

Even if visitation should unexpectedly rise, there is plenty of room to roam in the park's half-million acres of wilderness. And if the national park per se is not large enough, the park is linked with Lake Chelan and Ross Lake national recreation areas forming the "North Cascades Complex." These two large lakes, also under National Park Service dominion, plus surrounding National Forest wilderness, add up to a vast tract that would take a lifetime to explore.

Ross Lake is an inverted L-shaped body of water that divides the national park into north and south segments. Fjord-like Lake Chelan, cradled by Stehekin Valley, borders the park on the south.

The three national park areas—the park proper and the two lakes—are not easy country to hike. Learning that the national park has about 350 miles of maintained trail can make a hiker's heart flutter in expectation. However, many park trails are very long, suitable only for multi-day backpacking expeditions. Much of the park's vast high country is accessible only by difficult cross-country travel. Relatively few trailheads can be found along North Cascades Highway, the region's only paved road. Also, few trailheads begin right in the national park proper; many more begin in the bordering Ross Lake National Recreation Area, Lake Chelan National Recreation Area and surrounding National Forest lands.

North Cascades is one park where compulsive planners will likely enjoy their adventure more than their more spontaneous fellow hikers. North Cascades National Park particularly rewards those who have an itinerary and schedule. Some of the best hikes in the area require ferry boat rides and park service van shuttles. Because the summer hiking season is so short, considering these logistical arrangements in advance is critical.

The park's peaks and passes offer glorious views and are well worth the considerable effort required to ascend them. Easier trails lead along creeks and lakeshores and show a gentler side of the Cascades.

Certainly few have appreciated the North Cascade's gentler nature. Fur trapper-trailblazer Alexander Ross traversed these Cascades in 1814 and reported entering forests "almost impervious with fallen as well as standing timber." Complained Ross: "A more difficult route to travel never fell to man's lot."

The North Cascades are the glorious last act of a Cascade Range drama that plays from Northern California's Lassen Peak to British Columbia's Manning Park. Southern segments of the range take the form of a long plateau interrupted by such awesome volcanic peaks as Mt. Shasta, Mt. Hood and Mount St. Helens. In contrast, the North Cascades are not of volcanic origin and consist of jumbled clusters of alpine peaks. (A big volcano—Mt. Baker—is immediately west of the park, however.)

Ice, in the form of vast continental ice sheets and alpine glaciers, shaped the North Cascades. Glaciers formed the park's river valley, creating the characteristic high steep walls and wide U-shaped valley floors. Glaciers sculpted the ragged peaks and ridges, and gouged dozens of bowl-shaped basins known as cirques high on the mountains' shoulders.

North Cascades National Park was established in 1968 after one of the West's typically acrimonious and typically long battles (80 years) between resource extractors and environmentalists. North Cascades Highway was completed a few years after the park's founding and, combined with some excellent National Park Service and U.S. Forest Service efforts, has made the region an attractive one to visit. Attractive that is, to those in the know—and of course, few know.

North Cascades National Park remains a diamond in the rough—emphasis on rough. For the well-prepared hiker there are some extraordinary opportunities for solitude in this loneliest of national parks.

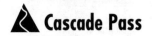 Cascade Pass

Cascade Pass Trail

To Cascade Pass is 7.5 miles round trip with 1,800-foot ele-
vation gain; to Sahale Arm is 11 miles round trip with
2,600-foot gain

How many switchbacks climb to the top of Cascade Pass? Don't ask. How's the view from up there?

Stupendous, in a word.

Hanging glaciers, high cliffs, a horizon of jagged peaks—the views from Cascade Pass and from farther along the crest at Sahale Arm are, in the opinion of many veteran Cascades hikers, among the best in the Pacific Northwest.

North Cascades Highway may very well live up to its hype as Washington's most scenic drive; however, while the drive may be one you'll long remember, this hike is one you'll never forget. In fact, even the trailhead parking lot boasts eye-popping vistas of glaciered mountains.

The hike to 5,423-foot Cascade Pass is a popular one, particularly among weekend warriors from Pugetopolis, but increasingly among out-of-state and foreign hikers. What was once a rugged route used by Native Americans and later by explorers and settlers has now, after much engineering, been rendered into a well-graded, wide pathway with a multitude of switchbacks. Experienced hikers accustomed to much steeper Cascade climbs feel slowed to a slug's pace by the endless zigzagging, but more casual hikers are grateful for the trail's user-friendly design.

The National Park Service trail construction works well at Cascade Pass; it protects the fragile meadow ecology and accommodates the hordes of hikers. (Quarter hordes, really—compared to other trails in North Cascades National Park this one is heavily used;

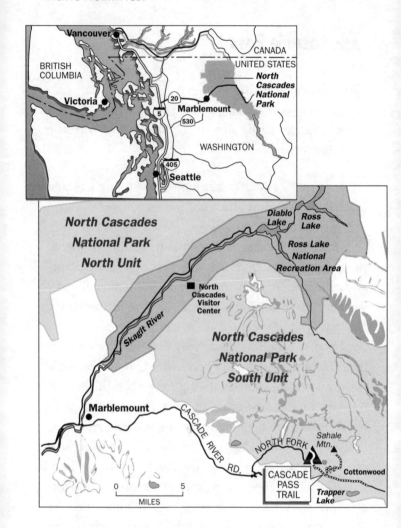

however, in comparison to other national parks, North Cascades receives few visitors.) Help protect the fragile subalpine vegetation by staying on the trail.

Anyway, don't be surprised if you find a dozen or so hikers on the pass when you surmount that last switchback. Truly, the National Park Service has thought of everything, you might muse up top as you note the self-composting toilet perched atop Cascade Pass.

The first two miles of trail gently switchback through the forest, then steepen as more switchbacks take you above timberline to open, glacier lily-bedecked meadows that offer increasingly good views.

Not as good as those from Cascade Pass, however. It's the greatest show on ice—Cascade Peak, the Triplets and the sometimes show-stopping performance of Johannesburg Mountain, whose hunks of glacial ice tumble from its shoulders to explode on the rocks below.

From the north side of the pass, ambitious hikers can head along the crest to Sahale Arm for equally awesome views that include Stehekin Valley. If you've made shuttle arrangements you can hike down from Cascade Pass 5.5 miles to Cottonwood Camp on Stehekin River Road.

Caution: Floods in 1995 destroyed significant portions of Stehekin Valley Road, especially above High Bridge. Check with the National Park Service concerning the status of this road and the availability of shuttle services.

Access: From State Route 20 in Marblemount, turn east on Cascade River Road (rather rough dirt) and follow it 22.3 miles to road's end and the trailhead.

 Thunder Creek

Thunder Creek Trail

To Fourth of July Trail Junction is 3.4 miles round trip; to McAlester Camp is 12 miles round trip; to Fourth of July Pass is 10 miles round trip.

It's a day hike or a backpack, a one-way or an out-and-back. It's a short saunter along the Thunder Creek Arm of Diablo Lake or a long north-south North Cascades traverse. However you hike it, Thunder Creek is a memorable trail.

Day-trippers find Thunder Creek Trail's first section a very pleasant ramble along the south side of Diablo Lake. At 1.7 miles the path intersects Fourth of July Pass Trail. Continuing, the path leads past shady picnic sites to McAlester Camp, six miles from the trailhead.

From the aforementioned junction, Fourth of July Trail switchbacks through the forest 3.3 miles to Fourth of July pass. Up top are views of Colonial and Snowfield peaks, as well as panorama of ice and sky.

Panther Creek Trail descends five miles through a handsome valley to North Cascades Highway. If you've made shuttle arrangements you've got yourself a great 10 mile one-way hike.

Access: Follow North Cascades Highway (20) to Colonial Creek Campground. Park in the lot above the boat ramp.

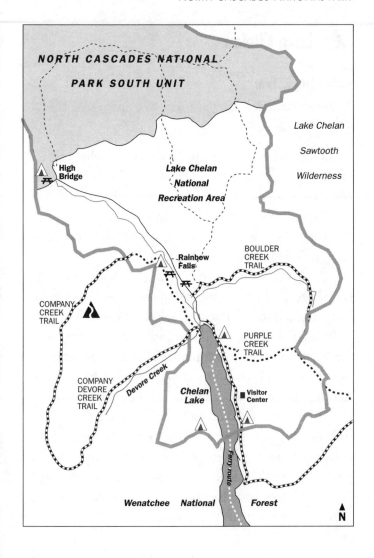

 Lake Chelan

Lakeshore Trail

To Moore Point is 7 miles one way; to Prince Creek is 17.2 miles one way.

If the lake is what you want, the lake is what you get on Lakeshore Trail, which has its share of hill-climbs, but never rises more than 500 feet above the lake.

Views? Good vistas of the ridges on the other side of the lake to be sure, but mostly of Lake Chelan, cold and clear, right below the trail.

Compared to other snowbound Cascade pathways, Lakeshore Trail has a long hiking season. It's among the first area trails to be snow-free, sometimes as early as May 1. Springtime, when wildflowers abound, and early summer are the best times on this trail. Later in the summer, the days are a bit too hot for comfortable hiking. Autumn, however, is a fine time for a lakeside ramble.

From its trailhead at Golden West Visitor Center, the path heads south along Chelan's northeast shore. After crossing through a forest of Douglas fir and ponderosa pine, the trail reaches the Lake Chelan National Recreation Area boundary and enters the Forest Service's Lake Chelan Sawtooth Wilderness.

Access: Moore Point, 7 miles out, is a good destination for a day hike. Arrange a boat pick up at Moore Point or at Prince Creek another 10 miles down the trail.

 **Stehekin Valley**

Stehekin Valley Trails
4 to 10.8 miles round trip.

For Puget Sound residents, waiting for, commuting by, and relying upon a ferry boat is part of the Pacific Northwest lifestyle. No big deal then to board a ferry for a hiking holiday.

While some Seattle adventurers might be a bit blasé about the aquatic mode of trailhead transport, few hikers from any part of the world are unmoved by walking the superb trails around Lake Chelan. Steep mountains rising 7,000 feet above the lake offer an awesome setting for ferry rides and hiking adventures.

Deep and dramatic Stehekin River Valley is the heart of Lake Chelan National Recreation Area.

When the glaciers that sculpted Stehekin Valley and Lake Chelan retreated, another ice sheet advanced to deposit a moraine at the lower end of the valley; this natural plug enabled the lake level to rise substantially. In 1928 the Chelan River was dammed, forming the Lake Chelan we see today. At 1,548 feet, it's one of the deepest lakes in the country.

It's possible to enjoy the lake for the day, although you won't have time to get in much hiking. The 51-mile boat trip to Stehekin Landing and the return trip use up much of the day. National Park rangers offer guided walks for those wishing to get a small taste of local flora and history.

The National Park's Golden West Visitor Center offers, maps, information, nature walks and evening talks, as well as North Cascades art exhibits.

A better bet is an overnight stay at one of the several shuttle bus accessible campgrounds located along Valley Road or at North Cascades Stehekin Lodge.

Despite all that water in Lake Chelan, the area around it isn't so wet. Its location is on the drier, eastern side of the Cascades.

Unlike the ferries that ply Puget Sound, the Lake Chelan Ferry carries no automobiles. When you arrive at Stehekin you must rely on shuttle bus transport (operated by the National Park Service) or private taxi service to reach campgrounds and most trailheads. The privately operated bus travels four times a day from Stehekin Landing to High Bridge. Shuttle service extends the length of Valley Road, some 18 miles to Cottonwood Camp and Cascade Pass trailhead. (Stehekin Valley Road was recently closed by storm damage; check on its status with the park.) If you're day hiking, be sure to carry a ferry schedule.

Some of the popular shorter Stehekin hikes include the 5-mile round tripper to Agnes Gorge and the 4-mile round trip jaunt from Cottonwood Campground to Horseshoe Basin. More than a dozen waterfalls cascade from snowfields onto this basin meadow.

Cascade Pass Trail (described from the west, Cascade River Road side earlier) is a 13.8 mile round trip hike from Flat Creek on the Stehekin Valley Road with a 2,600-foot elevation gain.

 Purple Pass

Purple Mountain Trail

To Purple Pass is 7.5 miles round trip with 5,700-foot elevation gain.

Purple Mountain Trail begins at Golden West Visitor Center. Unlike Lakeshore Trail, which makes every effort to stick close to Lake Chelan, Purple Mountain Trail appears to climb away from it in as short a time as possible.

Oh, what a climb! A zillion switchbacks (the park service officially reports only 57) lead to Purple Pass.

After your considerable uphill labors, reward comes in the form of little Lake Juanita and 7,372-foot Boulder Butte. The butte, a fire lookout site in the 1930s and 1940s, offers dizzying 360-degree views that take in the surrounding rugged peaks, Stehekin Valley and, of course, Lake Chelan.

Access: The signed trail begins at Golden West Visitor Center.

 Park Creek Pass

Park Creek Trail

To Five Mile Camp is 10 miles round trip; To Park Creek Pass is 16 miles round trip with 3,800-foot elevation gain.

Magnificent wildflower-strewn alpine meadows and close-up views of hanging glaciers are two of many compelling reasons to ascend Park Creek Pass, hiking highlight of the upper Stehekin River Valley.

Strong hikers can make the pass and return in a day, but a better bet is a two- or three- day backpacking trip. No camping is allowed in the fragile alpine meadow near the pass, but good campsites are available below the pass at Buckner and Five Mile Camps. You must obtain a free camping permit from the ranger stations or Visitor Center and camp only in designated sites.

Park Creek Pass is part of the Cascade Crest; from here, all western waters descend to Puget Sound, all eastern waters into Lake Chelan. Backpackers often continue another 19.4 miles west to Colonial Creek Campground, which adds up to a 27.4-mile one-way backpack.

From its shuttle bus serviced trailhead on Stehekin River Road, some 18.5 miles from Stehekin, the path climbs steeply into conifer-land, emerging at an overlook for a brief look-see at Stehekin Valley before dropping a half-mile to Two Mile Camp on Park Creek. After crossing a bridge over the creek, the trail resumes its ascent (not too strenuous, though) for three miles to Buckner and Five Mile Camps.

Park Creek Trail traverses alpine meadows as the valley widens. Above rise the awesome walls of Booker, Buckner, Storm King and Goode mountains. Leaving the valley, the path switchbacks two miles through the forest, rising above the trees a mile below the pass. A final mile's climb gains narrow, rocky, Park Creek Pass.

 Desolation Peak

Desolation Trail

From Desolation Landing to Desolation Peak is 13.6 miles round trip with 4,500-foot elevation gain.

The view from Desolation Peak lookout stays with you for a lifetime: in-your-face vistas of Hozomeen Mountain, Jack Mountain in the middle distance, the Picket Range and snowy Mt. Baker farther away to the west.

It was such a view that gave Beat-generation writer Jack Kerouac more than one mystical experience during the summer of 1956 when he served as a fire lookout atop Desolation Peak. The poet-novelist's time on the mountain inspired *Desolation Angels*, in which star angels dance over the great dark void beyond the lookout.

Apparently the mountains around here inspire visions. Sourdough Mountain Fire Lookout, located about 12 miles southwest of Desolation Peak, was staffed by Pulitzer Prize-winning poet Gary Snyder who has recounted his mountaintop experiences in poetry and prose.

The pathway to Desolation Peak may not offer heavenly inspiration but it's guaranteed to be a heck of a hike. Most hikers board the water taxi at Ross Lake Resort for a ride to Desolation Landing, near the mouth of Lightning Creek where it enters Ross Lake. The water taxi leaves Desolation-bound hikers at a spur trail which very shortly connects to the Desolation Trail. The first part of the hike is a mellow two miles along the lakeshore with East Bank Trail. Desolation Trail then begins a steep ascent, climbing from forest to meadows and rising high above Ross Lake. Next day your legs are sure to remember this ascent to the lookout (closed to the public) and the return to the lake.

Access: Follow State Route 20 to the trailhead for Ross Lake. Hike the path down to Ross Dam and Ross Lake Resort. Make arrangements for water taxi drop-off and pick up at Desolation Landing.

 Ross Lake

East Bank Trail

To Hozomeen Campground is 31 miles one way.

Ross Lake, formed by a dam on the Skagiit River, divides North Cascades National Park into north and south sections. While its purpose, along with Diablo and Gorge lakes and dams is hydroelectric—to supply juice to Seattle—its recreation potential is considerable.

Surrounding Ross Lake are more than 100,000 acres of thick forests, dramatic mountain peaks and enchanted valleys. A half-dozen major trails, including pleasant lakeshore rambles and strenuous peak climbs, explore Ross Lake National Recreation Area.

North Cascades Highway provides some access to the southern half of the recreation area. Access to the north sector is only possible through Canada via a road that leaves from Hope, British Columbia.

The best hike on the west side of Ross Lake is along 15-mile long Big Beaver Trail, which begins at Ross Dam. (The dam can be reached by hiking the Ross Dam Trail from North Cascades Highway or by ferry boat from Diablo.) After passing Ross Lake Resort, the path bends north through a mixed forest of Douglas fir, hemlock and cedar. Six miles out, the path reaches a footbridge spanning Big Beaver Creek. If you want to make this hike a one-way journey, the resort's water taxi service reaches Big Beaver Camp. (Make arrangements in advance at Ross Lake Resort in person or by phone.)

Three miles farther along Big Beaver Creek are grand old stands of red cedar. Some of the ancient trees measure 18 feet in diameter and are more than 1,000 years old.

Big Beaver Trail crests Beaver Pass, then intersects Little Beaver Trail. Backpackers enjoy making a 28-mile semi-loop by following Little Beaver Trail east along Little Beaver Creek to Ross Lake. Water taxi service can be arranged for either a drop-off or pick up at the Little Beaver trailhead on the lakeshore. Note: No trail travels the west shore of Ross Lake.

Ross Lake's no-less wild east shore is traveled by the appropriately named East Bank Trail. This path parallels the lakeshore for 20 miles or so. The way is fairly flat and offers conveniently spaced trail camps en route.

An excellent 31-mile backpack is the one-way jaunt from North Cascades Highway to Hozomeen Campground located near the Canadian border. Arrange a pickup with the water taxi service for your return from Hozomeen Campground. (Or convince someone to drive into British Columbia and pick you up from the camp.)

If you want to get your feet wet, so to speak, join East Bank Trail from its official trailhead on State Route 20.

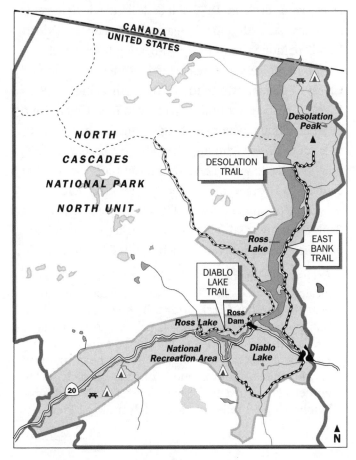

Descend 0.3 mile to the Ruby Creek Bridge where interpretive plaques tell the colorful story of an 1880s gold rush. From the bridge, East Bank Trail leads another 2.7 miles to a junction with Little Jack Mountain Trail.

For a formidable workout, tackle Little Jack's 54 switchbacks for the three-mile climb (and 4,000-foot elevation gain!) to a ridgetop saddle. Some hikers swear the views of the peak parade—Snowfield, Colonial, Pyramid and Crater—are worth the grunt while other hikers just swear. The trek from the highway to the top of Little Jack is 12 miles round trip.

A much easier way to go is to take the 0.8-mile spur trail leading to the Ruby Arm of Ross Lake. This adds up to a humane 7.5 mile round trip from the highway.

East Bank Trail crests a forested divide via Hidden Hand Pass. Back in 1879 miner Jack Rowley (remembered by Jack Mountain) imagined he saw a "Hidden Hand" pointing the way to gold-bearing Ruby Creek.

From the pass, the trail leads 12.2 miles to Lightning Creek (the latter two-thirds of the path alongside Ross Lake). A suspension bridge spans Lightning Creek. Here East Bank Trail junctions with Lightning Creek Trail, a 10-mile route along Lightning Creek that connects with five-mile long Willow Lake and Hozomeen trails that in turn connect to Hozomeen Camp at the Canadian border.

From the junction with Lightning Creek Trail, East Bank continues two miles along the lakeshore to a junction with Desolation Trail, which climbs Desolation Peak.

Access: A large parking area for East Bank Trailhead is located at mile post 138 on North Cascades Highway near the Panther Creek Bridge. By boat: Arrange boat transportation to Lightning Creek, Hozomeen Camp and other destinations around the lake by contacting Ross Lake Resort. East Bank Trail's northern trailhead at Hozomeen Campground on the Canadian/U.S. border can be reached from Hope, British Columbia byfollowing 40-mile long gravel Silver-Skagit Road.

Rainy Lake, Lake Ann

Rainy Lake National Recreation Trail

To Rainy Lake is 1.8 miles round trip; to Lake Ann is 4 miles round trip.

Unlike Oregon's Coast Highway 1 and the Columbia Gorge Scenic Highway, North Cascades Highway cannot boast of an inviting, easily accessible trailhead located every couple miles along the way.

The rambles to Rainy Lake and Lake Ann are an exception. In fact, the U.S. Forest Service has constructed a large attractive picnic area and such fine trails (the one to Rainy Lake is paved for wheelchair access and hikers of all abilities) that the whole family is compelled to stop and stretch car-cramped legs.

The walk to Rainy Lake offers a taste of the remote North Cascades wilderness. Lyall Glacier sheathes the slope above the lake, which resembles a classic Cascades' cirque. Adding to the magnificent alpine scene are a couple of waterfalls tumbling into the south end of the lake.

One of the more amusing Forest Service signs I've ever encountered is posted near the beginning of the trail to Lake Ann. It reads:

TRAIL BEYOND HERE IS STEEPER BUT VERY SCENIC.

That's as succinct a summation as any to describe the trail, which begins in forest, traverses a meadow and arrives at a junction 1.5 miles out. Follow the left fork to Lake Ann for sunbathing and trout fishing. For a taste of the country, follow the right fork 1.5 miles to Heather then Maple Pass for good views of Lake Ann and surrounding Cascade peaks.

For a splendid day hike, take the Maple Pass Trail and make an eight-mile loop.

Access: From North Cascades Highway (20) some 50 miles southeast of Marblemount, turn south on the short spur road to Rainy Pass Picnic Area.

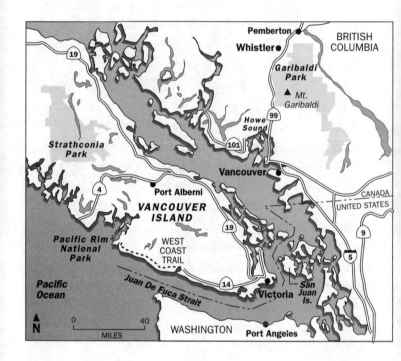

BRITISH COLUMBIA

Stanley Park, pride of Vancouver.

VANCOUVER

CHAPTER THIRTEEN

VANCOUVER

It's appeared in your living room a hundred times, but you probably don't know its name. The many faces of Vancouver can be seen frequently on television. Moviemakers have found the city and its environs to be a convincing substitute for a wide range of locales—Hong Kong, Seattle, Middle America, South America, China, Vietnam, the south of France and the American West.

"Hollywood North" is now third only to Los Angeles and New York in North American television and film production.

What is attractive to the filmmaker is equally compelling to the walker. Vancouver's locations are many and diverse: the city itself spreads over the Burrard Peninsula, its shoreline borders a Pacific Ocean inlet called the Strait of Georgia, the North Coast Mountains and outlying Fraser Valley farm lands nearby.

"Vancouver is one of the world's best cities for hiking because the wilderness is right in our backyards," declares Manfred Schollerman, owner-operator of Rockwood Adventures, a walking tour company. "A twenty-minute walk takes you from city streets into a rain forest with thousand-year old trees."

Visitors from Asia and Europe, whose cities are far, far from any wilderness, are particularly awestruck by the close proximity of the forest primeval to civic center, explains Schollerman. Indeed, his most popular jaunt, the Capilano River Canyon Walk begins near a shopping center and almost before his walkers can say "banana slug," they find themselves in a temperate rain forest.

Trails weave through an emerald forest of hemlock, red cedar and Douglas fir, over a forest floor carpeted with moss, ferns and flowering plants.

From the town's earliest days, Vancouverites vowed to keep their greenery close by. In 1886, the newly incorporated city's first resolution allowed purchase of a thousand acres of wooded peninsula from the Canadian government. Stanley Park, Canada's largest city park, includes not only cricket pitches and tennis courts, but forests and a rugged coastline.

Although it boasts an urban skyline—a modest collection of high-rises—Vancouver's skyline is really the local mountains, all the more dramatic for their precipitous rise from behind this city at water's edge. Grouse Mountain, Mt. Seymour, and Mt. Hollyburn beckon city-dwellers to climb their aerie heights, as do such intriguingly named summits as The Lions and Golden Ears.

Color Vancouver green—politically as well as geographically. Vancouver is the home of Greenpeace and headquarters for many other environmental groups struggling to preserve British Columbia's vast backcountry and ensure that the province remains faithful to its "Super. Natural." travel slogan. Conservationists want Vancouver to retain its super, natural look, too—a difficult task given the city's three percent annual growth rate. Both no-growthers and pro-growthers have nicknamed Vancouver "City of the Building Cranes."

Vancouver shares some surface similarities with Seattle—age, size and waterfront setting. The city carries on a mostly friendly rivalry with its Pacific Rim neighbor. But proud Vancouverites are quick to point out their city is far greener downtown and all around, and their waterfront is not cut off by freeways and industry like Seattle's.

The city itself numbers only a half-million people but outlying areas swell the Vancouver metro area population to 1.7 million. Vancouver neighborhoods offer some pleasant city walks—through Japantown, Little Italy and the urbane West End. Historically interesting Gas Town and the waterfront offer some fine excursions, too.

Vancouver's best walks, however, are on its wild side. The vast wilderness just beyond Vancouver's suburban sprawl is not the abstraction it is in North American metropolitan areas more cut off from the wild. Wilderness trailheads are located at the end of suburban streets. Just minutes from downtown coffeehouses is a mist-shrouded forest full of mountain lions and bears.

Vancouver's North Shore Rescue Team, a group of volunteers much admired for their efforts to locate hikers lost in the oh-so-close North Shore Mountains, is frequently dispatched during the summer hiking season.

Still, more and more Vancouverites and visitors are taking to the hills, and outdoor equipment and walking shoe stores abound. Every city-dweller, it sometimes appears, owns all the accoutrement required for a stylish saunter into the neighboring wild: a day pack, hiking boots, high-tech outerwear and one of those warm and fluffy garments known locally as "fuzzies."

Many city-slickers overestimate their backcountry skills, experts point out. While this situation exists in park land around every big city, the problem is more acute in Vancouver because the terrain is so rugged. More than a dozen hikers have perished in the North Shore Mountains during the last five years.

The North Shore Rescue Team advises nouveau mountaineers to pack a cell phone, figuring that the city is so close distressed hikers can call in and say, "Help, I'm lost, come and get me."

Perched on the edge of thousands of miles of wilderness, Vancouver is unique among North American cities. Most trails that explore the city's wild side are well-marked, and you won't need a cell phone unless you're calling for a post-hike dinner reservation.

 Granville Island

False Creek Trail
6.2-mile loop; shorter walks possible.

Vancouver's False Creek (actually a tidal inlet) was until 1970 little more than a dump, an open sewer. Then came a rapid renaissance. Industrial land on both sides of False Creek was reclaimed for waterfront shopping, dining, walking, living. As False Creek was restored, so was Granville Island, now one of Vancouver's major commercial and cultural centers.

Redevelopmentville, federally bankrolled no less, is usually an aesthetic disaster, but here they did it right. The False Creek-Granville Island walk is Vancouver's best urban jaunt. Follow the sea wall and some waterfront streets to visit a maritime museum, a science center, a brew pub, parks and shops.

Granville Island's public market features espresso bars, every kind of ethnic fast-fare from Greek to Thai to British (fish and chips), as well as flower stalls, fruit and vegetable stands. Slake your thirst with an all-natural unpasteurized beer at Granville Island Brewery, Canada's first microbrewery, established in 1984. Occasional tours are offered.

Ferry service (small charge) helps you customize a False Creek walk for your time and energy. If sightseeing is your primary objective, start at Granville Island, then walk the seawall.

If you want a 10K-see-it-all workout, start walking at the mouth of False Creek in Vanier Park. Drop by the flying saucer-looking H.R. MacMillan Planetarium, the Vancouver Museum (pioneer and native history exhibits) and the Maritime Museum. Follow the seawall to Granville Bridge and Granville Island, then head east along False Creek. At Cambie Bridge, the seawall ends and urban hikers detour inland for a few blocks through the last, real industrial area (unlikely to remain so for much longer). At the top of the False Creek inlet, visit Science World.

Rejoin the shoreline path and head back to the Cambie and Granville bridges. Take the Burrard Bridge back to the shore or board the ferry for the five-minute ride across False Creek.

Access: From the Granville Bridge, follow the signs to Granville Island. To reach Vanier Park from the north, cross Burrard Bridge and turn right on Cypress Street. Follow the signs to Vancouver Museum and Planetarium and its free parking lot. Two pay lots are in Vanier Park.

 Stanley Park

Sea Wall Trail

6.5-mile loop.

Vancouver's sprawling playground has the wide lawns, cricket pitches, picnic areas, and military monuments characteristic of a city park, but it's Stanley Park's wild side and ocean shore that attracts walkers. At the heart of the park, one of North America's largest city parks, is a dense forest laced with walking paths.

Much of the peninsula was logged in the 1860s and later it came under the administration of the military. Then, with what now appears to be incredible foresight, the newly incorporated city of Vancouver, population then a mere one thousand, convinced the federal government to give its military reserve to the city for a park. In 1888, Governor General Lord Stanley officiated at the dedication of his namesake pleasuring ground.

The Pacific all but encircles Stanley Park, and along ocean's edge are sandy beaches and a sea wall that offer a walk to remember. One of the best walks in the park in North America, and certainly the best overall walk in Vancouver is the walk along Stanley Park's seawall.

Saturdays, and especially Sundays, the sewall is a virtual parade route with in-line skaters and cyclists in one lane, baby strollers, joggers and walkers in the other. Power-walk the one-way, counterclockwise path in 90 minutes or stroll it in three hours.

From the foot of Georgia Street, you'll skirt the marina, then join the seawall, traipse past the Royal Yacht Club and pass a causeway leading to Deadman's Island, a one-time native burial site and now a Naval facility. You'll soon pass a more pleasant reminder of Vancouver's native inhabitants—the impressive totem poles carved by the Kwakwiutl and Haida in the late nineteenth century.

At mile-mark 2 is a children's water playground and

Lumbermen's Arch, and halfway along is the Lion's Gate Bridge. Rounding Prospect Point, the seawall curves southwest. On warm summer days you're sure to spot sunbathing Vancouverites at Third Beach and Second Beach. Side trails lead to Lost Lagoon, once swampland and now a bucolic body of water patrolled by coots and wood ducks and visited by Canadian geese and trumpeter swans. Improvise a route along the lagoon's south side back to the trailhead or continue along the seawall, and then a signed pedestrian path back to your starting point. The seawall continues several miles past Stanley Park.

Access: Metered parking is available inside Stanley Park, but if you can avoid driving into the park, particularly on busy summer weekends, do so. Note that vehicle traffic moves counterclockwise; use the Georgia Street entrance. By bus: Board the #14 Stanley Park/Downtown bus on Pender Street and disembark on Alberni Street. The park is only a 15-minute walk from downtown. The best entrances for the visitor afoot are Alberni Street or Beach Avenue.

 Capilano Canyon

Capilano Pacific Trail

From Ambleside Park to Cleveland Fish Hatchery is 4.7 miles one way.

If you have time for only one adventure on the urban edge, visit Capilano River Regional Park, located between North and West Vancouver. The river, cascading through the middle of the park, has carved a deep canyon in the granite.

The name Capilano may be familiar because of the famed Capilano Suspension Bridge (in my view Canada's most overrated tourist attraction, though many of the 600,000 a year who visit may feel more enthralled by the sight of the span.)

The trails on the west side of Capilano Canyon are free and more inspiring. And locals know if you keep walking there's an equally charming small wooden bridge over Capilano Canyon that's free.

Sixteen miles of trail lead through the park. The longest one is the 4.7-mile Capilano Pacific Trail which leads from Ambleside Park to Cleveland Dam and the Capilano Fish Hatchery.

This walk begins in West Vancouver, or West Van, as residents call their neighborhood bordered by the North Shore Mountains and the sea. Walkers in this bedroom community of quaint cottages, modern hillside homes and some mega-condos, ramble the 1.25-mile long seawall in Ambleside Park. The park is canine friendly: dogs have their own beach and their own paved runway along the seawall.

From the park the route passes behind the Park Royal Shopping Center, built on land owned by the native Capilano. The route passes under Highway 1, the Trans-Canada Highway, and under a railway bridge to reach the Capilano River mouth.

From May to September, salmon and trout battle Capilano's cascades as they swim up-river to spawn. At the mouth of the Capilano River, native people have long fashioned traditional fish traps. Salmon are diverted from their up-river swim into rock highways that direct them into roundabouts where they can't get out.

The path, a one-time logging railway, leads along the river. From a vista point, enjoy grand views of downtown Vancouver, the port's huge container cargo facilities, freighters and speedboats, as well as Stanley Park and its skyline of totem poles.

Next the path ascends into a forest of tall cedar and hemlock. Sword ferns, salal and huckleberries line the path which winds among enormous stumps (legacy of logging days) that now serve as nursery logs for plants, ferns and mosses.

The trail splits. One branch leads to the Capilano Fish Hatchery. Here coho and Chinook salmon, as well as steelhead trout are reared. Through a glass wall, you can watch the fish struggle up-river.

The other trail branch leads to the top of Cleveland Dam, which towers about 300 feet above the Capilano River to the south and forms Capilano Lake to the north. A path leads from the dam down to the fish hatchery.

Access: From Vancouver, drive north over Lions Gate Bridge. Head west on Marine Drive past the Park Royal Shopping Center and turn left into Ambleside Park. By bus: From downtown Vancouver, the #250 bus drops you off at Ambleside Park.

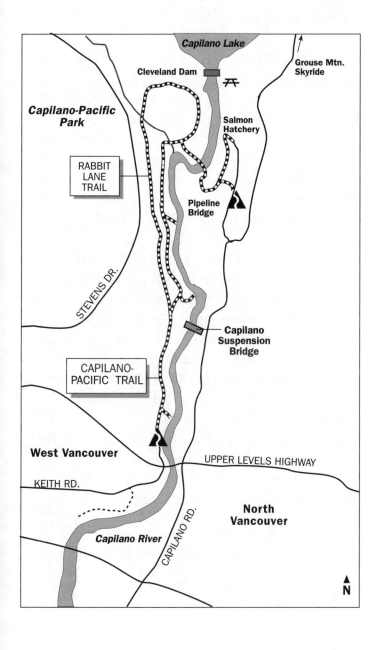

 Grouse Mountain

The Grouse Grind

To Grouse Mountain Plateau is 1.6 miles one way.

Why ride when you can hike? Sure the year-round Skyride swoops visitors to the top of 1,250-meter Grouse Mountain in just eight minutes.

But then you'd miss the challenge of the 45-degree climb from Grouse Mountain parking lot through beautiful woods to Grouse Mountain Plateau. Reward for the longest 1.6 miles you'll ever hike are panoramic views of the city, Vancouver Island and the Coast Mountains.

In winter, Grouse Mountain entices after-work skiers. During the summer, The Grind is more of a perverse fitness test than a nature trail for locals who tackle the mountain after work. The busiest nights are Wednesday and Thursday. Grouse Grinders meet at Bar 98 for a pitcher of draft and to swap tales of life and times (average hiking time is 90 minutes). Hikers then board a Skyride gondola for the ride down.

Locals measure their times up the mountain in early summer, then compare them with later efforts. Visitors will take their time (not measure it) on The Grind and smile at the crazy Canadians lurching past them.

Access: From downtown Vancouver, it's 7.5 miles north over Lion's Gate Bridge and Capilano Road to the ski lift. By bus: Board the #246 Highland westbound on Georgia Street, then transfer to the #232 Grouse at Edgemont and Ridgewood.

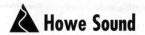 Howe Sound

Howe Sound Crest Trail

From Cypress Bowl to Porteau Cove is 18 miles one way with a 2,000-foot elevation gain.

Boaters know Howe Sound offers the best saltwater cruising north of San Francisco and, in the view of many, some of the best cruising in the world. Fishermen, looking to hook Chinook and coho, have made Howe Sound one of the most popular fishing spots on the Pacific Coast.

Hikers earn fabulous views of Howe Sound and the coastal mountains following the stunning 18-mile long Howe Sound Crest Trail. The path extends from Cypress Bowl in Cypress Provincial Park to Porteau Cove on the shore of Howe Sound.

As its name suggests, the path roughly follows a ridge crest that towers high above the sound shoreline. It flirts with some of Vancouver's famed summits, including Mount Brunswick, Mount Harvey and and particularly West Lion—one of the famed Lions Vancouverites are always pointing out. (From an easterly point of view, the two rugged summits do bear a resemblance to lions in repose.)

Only the best, most experienced hikers in terrific condition hike the whole trail in a day. Local hikers more commonly break the hike into two sections. Shorter hikes from either end of the trail also serve up some mighty fine scenery. Locals looking for shorter sound trails usually motor to Lions Bay and make for Unnecessary Mountain or the Mount Brunswick Trail.

Not-so-long-ago, before Highway 99 was built along the Howe Sound shoreline and before a road penetrated the Cypress Provincial Park area, the only way to the Lions and to peaks before it and beyond it was by foot from West Vancouver. Howe Sound Crest Trail is a partial revival of an old mountain footpath.

For all but Herculean hikers, the suggested trail route is northbound—that is, from the mountains to the sea. From the Cypress Park ski area the path gains 2,000 feet in elevation as it climbs Unnecessary Ridge. The trail tops out, some six miles from the trailhead, at the base of West Lion, at an elevation of about 5,000 feet. While the second two-thirds of the trail (12 more miles) does descend to sea level, it's by no means all downhill from The Lions. Expect numerous ups and downs.

To hike the whole route in one day requires sound physical condition and sound preparation. Bring lots of food and water. Keep an eye on the volatile weather. Rocky areas can be very slippery when wet. Because of lingering snow and avalanche danger, the hiking season is July to October, or until the first major snowfall.

Some stretches of trail are not well developed; however all of the trail is well-marked with orange paint on rocks, orange flags and orange metal markers.

Access: From West Vancouver, take the Upper Levels Highway west 10 miles to Cypress Bowl in Cypress Provincial Park. End point for the required car shuttle or pickup is Highway 99 at Porteau Cove, some 14 miles north of Horseshoe Bay.

VANCOUVER ISLAND

CHAPTER FOURTEEN

Vancouver Island

North America's largest island by far, 280-mile long, 80-mile wide Vancouver offers a Holland-sized haven for hikers. A mountainous backbone, a mellow east coast and majestic west coast, a rain forest, dramatic fjords, Pacific Rim National Park and dozens of provincial parks are some of the island's sights visited by footpaths.

Victoria is still a bit of olde England, still quaint after all these years, an oh-so-charming place for a carriage ride past the Parliament Building or a stop for a spot of tea at the Empress Hotel. However, if you'd rather step out into the great outdoors lifestyle instead of stepping into a late Victorian lifestyle, the city's proximity to memorable hiking, cycling and kayaking environments makes the area a recreational playground.

With the notable exception of world-famous West Coast Trail, the island's outdoorsiness remains a strictly locals-only pursuit. Hikers in the know make like the resident ramblers and look beyond the tea rooms of downtown Victoria to the southern isle's two dozen coastal parks and hundreds of miles of trails.

Just as the island impresses with its size, so does Victoria, the fourth-largest city in western Canada behind Vancouver, Edmonton and Calgary. Some 300,000 people reside in the provincial capital and its attendant suburbs.

Victoria cannot be said to hustle or bustle, though the oft-repeated jab at the place—"the world's only cemetery with a business district"—seems a bit exaggerated these days. With the warmest winter weather in Canada, it's refuge for seniors from colder climes and an increasingly popular place for Canadians to retire.

It simply moves at a slower pace—which makes it perfectly suited for walks, short and long, past architectural landmarks, historic homes, fabulous gardens and parks. Walk around the city's center, past large flower baskets hanging from the lamp posts. Amble the waterfront esplanade, one of North America's finest. Yachts and sea planes tie up in the harbor as do the ferries which dock right downtown. Musicians and street performers of all kinds add to the engaging scene.

Stroll over to Beacon Hill Park, a triumph of late nineteenth-century landscape architecture. Meander paths to rhododendron-ringed Fountain Lake, then enjoy a walk along the park's undeveloped coast.

Don't miss a visit to the British Columbia Provincial Museum, a kind of smaller scale Smithsonian with wonderful exhibits portraying the rain forest, the native inhabitants and European settlement. The museum offers a wonderful introduction to the habitats and history of the province, and adds to the walker's appreciation of the island.

Once outside the tidy confines of Victoria, getting to know Vancouver Island means getting to know the land. A rugged land it is, with a massive median strip of mountains extending the length of the island. Snow falls on such 7,000-foot plus peaks as Golden Hinde, Elkhorn and Victoria, offering supposedly snow-escaping Victoria residents a chance to see and ski it. Strathcona Provincial Park protects the high peaks, as well as Comox Glacier, the island's last remaining ice field, and Della Falls, one of Canada's highest waterfalls.

The isle's mountain massif separates two coasts as different as night and day. Vancouver's "inside" or eastern coast is home to some mellow communities and seascapes. The island's west coast has rugged terrain that discourages settlement, but beckons adventurous hikers.

The island's spine-spanning road, Highway 4, was

originally named the Alberni Colonization Road, part of a government effort to encourage settlement of the west coast. Wet weather stopped all but the hardiest, though both logging and fishing communities took advantage of the rich resources.

The island's west or "outside" coast boasts two trails —the already very well known West Coast Trail—and the newly completed Juan de Fuca Marine Trail.

Local environmentalists met with surprising success considering the predominant provincial paradigm, "Log first, ask questions later." One conservation success story is Carmanah Valley, where some of the world's largest spruce and cedar thrive. The Nitinat Lakes area, a triangle of tall trees above the West Coast Trail, was saved from the logger's ax by the Sierra Club and other Canadian conservationists during the island's epic eco battle of the 1970s.

Vancouver Island's inspiring west coast beckons beach walkers from near and far.

East Sooke Regional Park

Coast Trail

From Aylard Farm to Iron Mine Bay is 12.5 miles one way.

Imagine black bears roaming coastal headlands just miles from genteel Victoria. This is Vancouver's wild west coast, a wilderness located a short ride from the tea rooms and the fine hotels.

Some 40 miles of trails crisscross East Sooke Regional Park, a diverse preserve of rocky ridges, rain forest and rugged coastline. Springtime is when the buttercups bloom, along with monkeyflowers, orange honeysuckle and a host of other wildflowers. And summertime is when killer whales nose into the park's coves.

The park's most popular spot is onetime apple orchard, Ayland Farm, which offers picnicking, a sandy beach and swimming. It's also the park's major trailhead.

A favorite 7.5-mile loop of local hikers leaves Ayland Farm, climbs Babbington Hill via Babbington Hill Trail, heads straight for the Strait of Juan de Fuca, then joins the Coast Trail at Cabin Point for the return to the trailhead. Note that the park's interior is cut by many old roads and trails, sometimes making navigation difficult. A park map helps—somewhat.

For an adventure to remember, try the 12.5-mile Coast Trail, which extends from Ayland Farm to Iron Mine Bay. You'll need to arrange a car shuttle for the hike which takes about seven hours in wet weather, five hours in dry. Elevation gain and loss is minimal.

Coast Trail highlights include craggy headlands, forests of cedar, Douglas fir, western hemlock and Sitka spruce, as well as grand views of the Strait of Juan de Fuca and the Olympic Peninsula.

Access: Entry to the park is off either East Sooke Road or Gillespie Road.

Goldstream Provincial Park

Arbutus Loop, Goldstream, Prospectors Trails
0.5 to 3.7 miles round trip.

Just 12 miles from downtown Victoria is Goldstream, a provincial park with mighty trees and impressive water-falls. Sunlight slants through narrow openings in the tall tree canopy to light a world of alders, maples and flow-ering dogwood, as well as a multitude of ferns. Trails weave through a forest of Douglas fir and red cedar.

Arbutus Loop Trail and Arbutus Ridge Trail explore the habitat of Canada's only broad-leafed evergreen. The arbutus, characterized by its curious, thick, leathery leaves and reddish trunk with peeling bark, grows only on Vancouver Island and B.C.'s southwest coast.

Goldstream River was named by optimistic gold prospectors. Today, the real riches of the stream are its fish. From late October through December, thousands of salmon—chum, coho, and Chinook—enter the river from the Pacific via Finlayson Arm. The spawning salmon draw thousands of spectators, who learn more about the fish, as well as surrounding forest and foot-paths, at Freeman King Visitor Center, reached by trail from the north end of the picnic area parking lot.

The upper leg of Goldstream Trail parallels the Goldstream River, passing large trees, and visits 25-foot Goldstream Falls. Goldmine Trail leads past gold rush-era diggings, and crosses Niagara Creek to the brink of 156-foot Niagara Falls.

Prospectors' Trail (3.7 miles), which offers the longest tour of the park, tours the Douglas fir forest alongside Goldstream River and the oak and arbutus woodland on higher slopes.

Access: Leave Victoria on Route 1 (Island Highway) and drive 12 miles to Goldstream Provincial Park. The day use area entry is near the junction of the highway and Finlayson Arm Road.

Juan de Fuca Marine Trail Park

Juan de Fuca Marine Trail

30 miles one way.

Just south of the world famous West Coast Trail is another west coast footpath—the new Juan de Fuca Marine Trail. The path, which traces the Pacific shore of the Strait of Juan de Fuca, offers a superb sampling of Vancouver Island's rugged beauty, including forested cliffs, meandering creeks and tidepools.

European explorers had long been enchanted by the notion of a great strait giving passage from the New World to the Orient ever since 1592 when pilot Juan de Fuca claimed he and his Spanish shipmates located the fabled "Strait of Anian." Some historians believe de Fuca (actually Greek navigator Apostolos Valerianos) did indeed locate the strait that bears his Spanish alias; his claim to have sailed through the strait to the Atlantic Ocean and then back to Acapulco in 20 days does, however, detract from his credibility.

Captain Cook arrived in a fog in 1778 and found no strait at all. Captain Charles William Barkley did find the strait at 48 degrees, 30 minutes North Latitude and is often credited with its discovery, or at least rediscovery. Followup voyages by Spaniards, Americans and Englishman George Vancouver determined that, alas, the Strait of Juan de Fuca extends into North America a mere hundred miles.

Although the strait was not the shortcut to Asia hoped for by shippers, it did become a significant sea lane. Hardly a peaceful passageway, the strait's tides and intemperate weather have wrecked hundreds of ships, earning its waters the nasty nickname of "The Graveyard of the Pacific."

Today, even with the most modern navigational aids, negotiating the frequently fog-bound strait can be

Bridges and ladders lead through the lush coastal forest.

difficult. Still, more than a thousand vessels a month carrying cargo to and from the Pacific Rim pass through the strait. In come Toyota automobiles, out go Douglas fir logs through the ports of Seattle, Tacoma and Vancouver.

The Strait of Juan de Fuca separates two large continents and links North America by sea lane to the peoples and flourishing economies of the Pacific Rim.

Hikers may spot gray whales migrating between Bering Sea feeding waters and Baja California calving waters. Resident orcas pursue salmon through the strait.

Boosters of the new trail claim that many miles of the Juan de Fuca are indistinguishable from the West Coast Trail. There is some truth to this comparison; equally true, is that for the Juan de Fuca to grow in stature it will have to stand on its own merits. BC Parks is steward of the trail, which was completed in 1996.

For a moderate day hike of about four hours, hike down-coast from the rich tidepools of Botanical Beach to Parkinson Creek. If you can arrange a car shuttle, the 13.6-

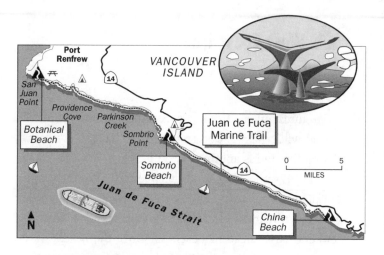

mile length between Botanical Beach to Sombrio Beach is one of North America's most engaging coastal hikes.

Access: Botanical Beach Park is located 1.5 miles south of Port Renfrew.

233

 West Coast Trail

West Coast Trail

47 miles one way.

It lures hikers from five continents. The dramatic coastal wilderness is one reason. The challenge of completing the trail is another.

The 47-mile long route between Port Renfrew and Bamfield is a melange of forest trails, beach, and low-tide sidewalk of sandstone at water's edge. Bold headlands bookend large crescent beaches. Above the beaches are coastal slopes forested with Sitka spruce, western red cedar and western hemlock.

Wildlife abounds: bear in the forest, bald eagles roosting on shoreline snags, plenty of pesky raccoons and mice. Sea otters and whales are often spotted offshore.

Two major rivers and more than 30 creeks cascade from the coastal slopes into the ocean. Bridges and cable cars span many of the creeks; ferry service shuttles hikers across the Nitinat Narrows and Gordon River.

What is now one of the premier recreation paths in North America was conceived as a "Life-Saving Trail" in order to provide shipwrecked sailors an escape path to civilization.

During the late 19th century, dozens of ships attempting to slip into the Strait of Juan de Fuca wrecked instead on west coast reefs. Hundreds were lost in the surf; even sailors who reached shore were likely to perish from the elements before reaching safety.

In 1890, the Canadian government built a rugged route linking Port Renfrew to Bamfield and strung a telegraph line from tree to tree to link the two hamlets. After the 1906 wreck of the S.S. *Valencia* when 126 passengers died, the trail was upgraded, suspension bridges were built over creeks, and shelters were equipped with telephones.

Increasingly sophisticated navigation and communication equipment, along with improved air-sea rescue techniques eliminated the need for the "Shipwreck" Trail. But hikers discovered it, and in 1970 the path, now called the West Coast Trail, along with the coastal slope was placed under the protection of Pacific Rim National Park.

The southern trailhead is Port Renfrew, slowly transitioning from logging industry to travel industry.

Port Renfrew is a 66-mile drive from Victoria, and a fee is charged for parking. A private bus line, the West Coast Trail Connector (Knight Limousines) services Port Renfrew. To reach the actual beginning of the trail, a ferry ride across the San Juan River is necessary.

The northern trailhead is the fishing hamlet of Bamfield. From Victoria, you can drive to Port Alberni on paved road then tackle the 56-mile dirt road to Bamfield. Or you can take the ferry from Port Alberni to Bamfield.

While the West Coast Trail still enjoys (if that's the right word) a reputation as one of the continent's most grueling treks, trail upgrades have made it less arduous. It remains a challenge to the average hiker, but is no longer only the province of hardy mountaineers.

Still, the park service's "West Coast Trail Preparation Guide" has enough caveats to stop even the most experienced hikers in their tracks: "Do not attempt to cross Adrenaline Surge Channel. People have died there!" or "Don't throw anything at a bear—it may provoke an attack."

The park map highlights evacuation sites. Difficulties facing hikers include mud and muck, high rivers, high tides, rogue waves, and fallen trees. More than 100 inches of rain a year falls on the trail. Even when it's not raining, expect everything—logs, rocks, sand and trail—to be wet.

Overcoming the considerable obstacles, more than 2,000 hikers trek end-to-end each year. Most hikers take a week (five to seven days) to complete the trail. Creekside campsites and driftwood for campfires are plentiful.

In addition to all the usual wet-weather preparations, hikers should carry a tide table and the West Coast Trail map that shows which beaches and points are passable at low tide. Park wardens recommend that each party carry a 45-foot length of rope for crossing creek mouths, or to facilitate rescue.

Because of the complex logistics to reach the trailhead, the West Coast Trail doesn't really lend itself to day hikes (unlike neighboring Juan de Fuca Trail). If you're out for a (long) day, begin at the Bamfield Trailhead and hike south six miles from the Pachena Bay Information Center to Pachena Point Lighthouse (location of a bed-and-breakfast). This is nice walking on uncharacteristically wide trail. For a truer taste of the West Coast Trail, continue another mile or so over the narrower, muddier pathway to the beach at the mouth of Michigan Creek.

Many hikers prefer to hike southwest to northeast, thus surmounting the more difficult half of the trail first.

Hike highlights: include the cable car crossings of Camper Creek, Cullite Creek and Walbran Creek, the beach walk beyond Vancouver Point, the cable car crossing at Carmanah Creek and a visit to Carmanah Lighthouse, the ferry across Nitinat Narrows, a hike through a rock arch near Tsuquadra Point, magnificent Tsusiat Falls, and cable car crossings of the Klanawa and Darling rivers.

GARIBALDI PROVINCIAL PARK AND WHISTLER

CHAPTER FIFTEEN

WHISTLER AND
GARIBALDI PROVINCIAL PARK

Whistler, often ranked as the number one ski resort in North America, put the stunning British Columbia Coast Range on the map; adjacent Garibaldi Provincial Park, 474,000 acres of forests, glaciers and alpine lakes, comprises most of the map.

Skiers know Whistler boasts North America's longest vertical run and the continent's best summer skiing. Hikers know Garibaldi Provincial Park as a vast land of alpine lakes and volcanic peaks. The park, located a mere 40 miles north of Vancouver, is named after 8,787-foot Mt. Garibaldi, one of many tall mountains in the range.

Farther south, the words "Coast Range" often conjure up images of the sunbaked ridges and palm-fringed shores of Southern California, the redwoods of Northern California or the rainy world of the Oregon Coast. The Pacific Ocean is usually nearby—a dominating influence. British Columbia's Coast Range, however, is an altogether different world of dense forests, snowy mountains, and even glaciers. Grizzly and black bears, mountain goats and wolverines roam the range.

Douglas fir, western hemlock and red cedar cloak the park's lower slopes. Alpine meadows are splashed with such seasonal blooms as lupine, snow lily, Indian paintbrush and western anemone.

Thirty-six miles of trail explore the park's backcountry, accessible from trailheads off Highway 99 between Squamish and Whistler. Garibaldi Lake/Black Tusk and Diamond Head are the primary backpacking destinations. Singing Pass, Cheakamus Lake, and Wedgemont Lake are other favorites.

Two hike-in campgrounds are located at Garibaldi Lake, an excellent place to establish a base camp for exploration of the surrounding area. From the lake, venture to Helm Lake, Panorama Lake, Mimulus Lake and Black Tusk, a dramatic, severely eroded volcanic peak.

In the Diamond Head area, a seven-mile trail leads to Elfin Lake where there's camping as well as an A-frame shelter that sleeps 30.

Some hikers, particularly day hikers, will enjoy making Whistler, with every apres-hike amenity, their base of operations. Other hikers might find the resort too pricey for their tastes, and the crush of trendy jet-setting skiers a bit much. All will agree, however, that pedestrian-only Whistler Village and environs is extremely walker-friendly.

Whistler has evolved into a year-round resort with lots of summer activities, including a concert series featuring jazz, bluegrass and classical music festivals. One of the best summer activities is hiking; there are some great walks right out of Whistler Village.

They're a bit helicopter crazy up here. Along with heli-skiing, heli-fishing and heli-rafting, there's heli-hiking. If you don't want one of the Whistler whirly-birds to take some of the uphill out of your hike, you can always ride the Blackcomb or Whistler Mountain ski lifts to several trailheads. Popular trails lead to Singing Pass and Rainbow Falls. From Whistler, Valley Trail leads to five lakes.

Garibaldi Lake, Black Tusk

Garibaldi Lake Trail

To Garibaldi Lake is 11.2 miles round trip with 2,700-foot elevation gain; to Black Tusk is 15 miles round trip with 5,800 foot elevation gain.

Mountain peaks, lakes and wildflower-festooned alpine meadows are some of the attractions awaiting the hiker who traverses this memorable land shaped by fire and ice. Two of the provincial park's most prominent features—Garibaldi Lake and Black Tusk—are accessible from a single trailhead and by trails that are themselves memorable.

Garibaldi Lake is a fine day's walk or an excellent place to establish a base camp for further exploration of this magnificent country. Splendid campsites are perched on the hillside above the lake. A few wooden platforms keep you, your tent and gear higher and drier than the sometimes soggy ground. Floating just offshore are the lake's Battleship Islands, a rocky archipelago connected by wooden bridges to the mainland.

Heroic hikers might reach the lake and Black Tusk in a single long day but the destinations are best divided into two daylong hikes or a longer backpacking trip. Another option is a one-way backcountry tour from Garibaldi Lake to Black Tusk, then out Helm Creek Trail to Cheakamus Lake. (See Cheakamus Lake Walk.)

Black Tusk, a pillar of volcanic rock, looms over the surrounding forest. No other Coast Range peak is as prominent and, in the right light, it's a downright forbidding-looking place. Native Squamish believed Thunderbird dwelled atop Black Tusk; lightning bolts came from the great bird's eyes whenever a human dared to climb too close. Perhaps Thunderbird's powers lingered because the summit was not conquered by mountaineers until 1912.

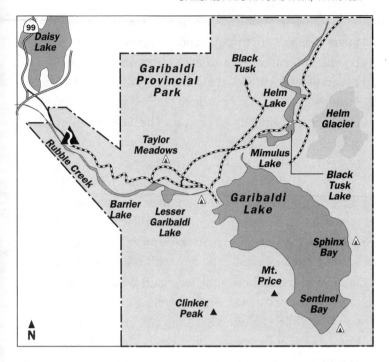

The view from the trailhead is something special. A red volcanic rock wall named The Barrier is a photographer's delight at sunset. The Barrier formed when molten lava met a glacier and was chilled and quickly hardened. This lava is the same stuff that formed the basin that now holds Garibaldi Lake.

The trail to the lake winds among Douglas fir and red cedar along the north side of Rubble Creek, whose banks are strewn with avalanche-deposited boulders. You might wonder, given the rather scanty outflow from Garibalid Lake, why Rubble Creek is so frothy and vigorous. Geologists say that waters from Garibaldi Lake, as well as from Lesser Garibaldi Lake, percolate through the porous volcanic rock then return to the surface as springs that in turn feed the creek.

About 3.5 miles out, the trail splits. The left fork leads to Taylor Campground and Black Tusk, Garibaldi Lake-bound hikers choose the right fork, which leads to a grand viewpoint (itself a fine destination for a shorter day hike) then another two miles to the lake.

From Garibaldi Lake, a half-hour's walk through the forest brings you to a junction with the Black Tusk-bound path coming from Taylor Meadows. An ascent on either of two parallel trails brings you to Black Tusk Meadows, which offers excellent picnicking and a view of climbers struggling up Black Tusk. The meadow affords a splendid range of options. You can head for Helm Lake or even Cheakamus Lake, nine miles away.

Black Tusk is a very vigorous two-mile climb. You'll ascend through alpine meadows, then across talus slopes to reach the mountain's prominent ridge. Many hikers will savor the view from here and return. The most experienced, preferably in company with other experienced mountaineers, will continue westward under the mountain's vertical south wall. Pass several rock chimneys until you reach the last one and trail's end. Using the fairly numerous handholds, carefully climb some 300 vertical feet to the top. Enjoy the fantastic views of the park before you make your ever-so-careful descent.

Access: From Highway 99, some 20 miles past Squamish and 12 miles short of Whistler, turn north on the signed BC Parks road and follow it 1.5 miles to the Garibaldi Lake/ Black Tusk parking lot.

 Cheakamus Lake

Cheakamus Lake Trail

To Cheakamus Lake is 4 miles round trip; to Singing Creek Camp is 8 miles round trip; to Helm Lake is 15 miles round trip with 2,700-foot elevation gain.

The Cheakamus Lake Trailhead, like better-known Garibaldi Lake Trailhead to the south, offers a range of hikes from easy walks to weekend backpacking trips.

Mostly level Cheakamus Lake Trail is a family-friend-ly outing. En route to the lake, you'll find a cool, mossy

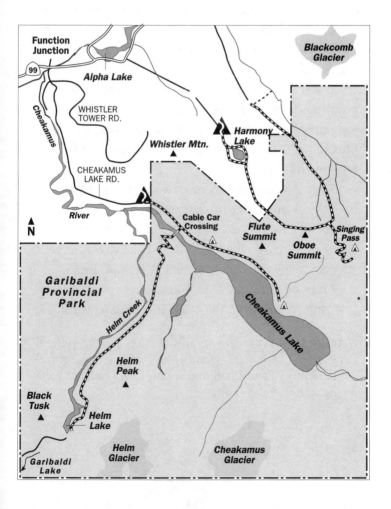

243

forest of Douglas fir, cedar and western hemlock. The route leads above the Cheakamus River, whose headwaters arise in the heart of Garibaldi Provincial Park. Wooden boardwalks and bridges help hikers keep their boots dry while crossing wet areas.

Emerging from the old-growth forest, you'll behold the lake, surrounded by a dramatic backdrop of glaciated summits. Meltwater from McBride Range ice fields fill the lake which, as you might imagine, offers mighty chilly swimming.

More pleasurable Cheakamus activities are fishing (rainbow trout and Dolly Varden char) and camping at the attractive sites located above the lakeshore. Some hikers like to pack in small inflatable boats in order to explore the lake and get an unbeatable view of Mt. Davidson, Overlord Mountain and the other peaks ringing the lake.

If you can tear yourself away from Cheakamus Lake, travel the fern-lined path above the lake's north shore. Abundant wildflowers from blue lupine to orange paintbrush color the scene, though do watch out for the equally abundant nettle.

Singing Creek and its modest trail camp, two miles from Cheakamus Lake, is your turnaround point.

Helm Creek Trail, which begins a mile from the Cheakamus Lake Trailhead, is definitely worth your attention. Follow it 1 mile to Helm Creek Bridge.

Once on the other side you can continue to Helm Lake and connect with the Black Tusk Trail network.

Access: From Highway 99 at the south end of Whistler, turn left (southeast) on narrow, gravel Cheakamus Lake Road and follow it 3.7 miles to the Cheakamus Lake Trailhead.

 **Diamond Head**

Elfin Lakes Trail

To Elfin Lakes is 14 miles round trip.

Looming over Cheakamus River Valley is the impressive ridge known as Diamond Head. The ridge has been deeply grooved by a retreating glacier, part of which still resides on Diamond Head's slopes. Here among the high peaks, the scene is distinctly alpine—a touch of the Swiss Alps in the southwest corner of Garibaldi Provincial Park.

The goal of this walk is Elfin Lakes, onetime site of Diamond Head Chalet, a log lodge operated by enterprising Norwegians from the 1940s to the late 1960s. Nordic skiers in winter and hikers in the summer take simple and snug shelter in a Ministry of Parks-constructed cabin built right next to the old lodge. As many as 30 hikers can snooze in bunkbed-style accommodations. If you want to sleep under the stars, there's a large meadow campsite above the little lakes.

The two small Elfin Lakes, one providing a drinking water supply, the other wash water, are overshadowed by the memorable surrounding scenery. They are, however, a worthy destination for a day's hike or for setting up a base camp for further exploration of the provincial park. From the lakes, hikers can continue to Opal Cone, a fragmented volcano or on to Mamquam Lake.

The way to Elfin Lakes is via an old, access road that ascends at a very mellow grade. Families, or those looking for a shorter hike should consider the five-mile round trip hike to Red Heather Day Shelter, a pretty, but often bug-infested picnic area.

Access: From Highway 99 in Garibaldi Provincial Park, take the Diamond Head exit and follow the access road 10 miles east to the parking area. Only the first 2.5 miles are paved; the balance of Mamquam Road is gravel.

 Whistler Mountain

Musical Bumps Trail

To Oboe Summit is 7.5 miles round trip with 1,000-foot elevation gain.

During the colder two-third's of the year Whistler Mountain is the exclusive domain of skiers. But near the end of May, the sun melts snowbanks, uncovering a network of footpaths. From late spring through early autumn, the mountain's grandeur is best explored in hiking, not ski boots.

Locals celebrate this change of seasons with their annual "Great Snow, Earth, Water Race" held up on Whistler Mountain and down in Whistler Valley. The top-to-bottom race features seven-member teams comprised of a downhill skier, a Nordic skier, a pair of cyclists to circle Alta Lake, a pair of canoeists to paddle down the River of Golden Dream to Green Lake and finally a runner to sprint for the finish line in Whistler Village.

From 1915 until the 1960s when the words Whistler and skiing became synonymous, summer was high season. Visitors came to fish and to relax at one of the valley's rustic lodges. After a period of quiet Whistler summers, the warm season is back big-time with tennis, golf, cycling and hiking.

From June to October, it's the hiker's turn to board the Whistler Mountain Express and ride the gondola up the mountain. After a 20-minute ride and a heady elevation gain of 3,818 feet, you disembark to find an array of beckoning trails at your feet.

If you're aim is a walk, not a hike, consider the mile-long Paleface Trail. This path drops below Roundhouse Lodge and loops back under the Express. Benches en route offer places to rest and contemplate the considerable view: Rainbow Mountain, Mt. Sproatt and grassy, wildflower-dotted Whistler Mountain itself. Another easy pathway is the short loop around nearby Harmony Lake, a sometimes snow-covered, sometimes boggy lakelet greatly reduced by runoff.

Boarding the Express isn't absolutely necessary to climb Whistler Mountain. You can join the five-mile long service road for the steep climb from Whistler Village.

The best longer day hike from the upper Express station is the Musical Bumps Trail which climbs a long ridge in adjacent Garibaldi Provincial Park. Your reward for scaling the musical summits are vistas of Cheakamus Lake, Black Tusk and an eyeful of the park's peaks and valleys. The Ridge Trail marches up and over the Musical Bumps—Piccolo, Flute and Oboe. Piccolo, first of the bump summits, is sufficiently inspiring for the casual hiker, while more gung-ho adventurers will continue to Oboe Summit, perched over Singing Pass.

If you've made the proper logistical arrangements, descend to Singing Pass for an alternate descent of Whistler Mountain. Otherwise return the gondola station and, depending on the state of your knees, ride or hike back to Whistler Village.

Access: Purchase a ticket for the Whistler Mountain Express at the lower station and enjoy the ride.

 Whistler Valley

Valley Trail

From Whistler Village, enjoy 6.2-mile and 9-mile loops; shorter walks are possible.

Sure Whistler Mountain commands the most visitor attention, but Whistler Valley is becoming an increasingly popular place to play. Valley Trail tours the flatlands, linking five lakes, seven parks, the village and the train station.

In winter, Valley Trail is a Nordic ski route; in summer, a walking and cycling path. Valley Trail has been extended in recent years and now totals more than nine miles in length.

Whistler Village is the hub for the mostly paved, mostly level trail that travels through a collage of scenes from historic cabins to the Whistler Tennis Club. Many of the sights to see en route are as attractive as their names —Rainbow Park, Green Lake and River of Golden Dreams.

The trail visits five lakes—Alpha, Nita, Alta, Lost and Green—each includes a picnic site. Lost Lake was once an isolated destination popular with au naturel swimmers; now it's easy to reach and most swimmers suit up.

The 10-kilometer loop of choice begins at the village and heads north on a clockwise tour past the Whistler Golf Club, travels by the River of Golden Dreams to Meadow Park, then across the highway to Green Lake, south to Lost Lake, and finally back to the village.

Access: From Whistler Village, join signed Valley Trail on the west side of Highway 99. From the Conference Center, take the underpass toward the Whistler Golf Club.

CONTACTS

OREGON

Oregon Coast

Oregon State Parks & Recreation
1115 Commercial Street N.E.
Salem, Oregon 97310
(503) 378-6305

Oregon B & B Directory
P.O. Box 1283,
Grants Pass, OR, 97526
(800) 841-5448

Rogue River

Siskiyou National Forest
Gold Beach Ranger District
1225 S. Ellensburg Ave.
Gold Beach, Oregon 97444
(503) 247-6651

U.S. Bureau of Land Management
Medford District
3040 Biddle Road
Medford, Oregon 97404
(503) 770-2200

U.S. Bureau of Land Managment
Rand Visitor Center
14355 Galice Road
Merlin, Oregon 97532
(503) 479-3735
(Open May 15-October 15)

Rogue River Reservations Inc.
Box 548
Gold Beach Oregon
(503) 247-6022,(503) 247-6504

Paradise Bar Lodge,
P.O. Box 456
Gold Beach, Oregon 97444
(800) 525-2161.

Crater Lake National Park

Crater Lake National Park
P.O. Box 7
Crater Lake, OR 97604
(503) 594-2211

Crater Lake Lodge
(503) 594-2511 (summer)
(503) 830-8700 (winter).

Three Sisters Wilderness

Sisters Ranger District
U.S. Forest Service
P.O. Box 249
Sisters, OR 97759
(541) 549-2111

Sisters Area Chamber of Commerce
P.O. Box 430
Sisters, OR 97759
(541) 549-0251

Mount Hood

Mt. Hood Information Center
65000 E. Highway 26
Welches, OR 97067
(503) 622-3191 (Local)
(503) 666-0704 (Portland)

Mt. Hood National Forest
Supervisor's Office
2955 N.W. Division Street
Gresham, OR 97030
(503) 666-0700

Timberline Lodge
(800) 547-1406

Hood River County Chamber of Commerce
(800) 366-3530

Columbia Gorge

Columbia River Gorge National Scenic Area
Waucoma Center
902 Wasco Avenue, Suite 200
Hood River, OR 97301
(541) 386-2333

Bonneville Dam's Bradford Island Visitors Center
(503) 374-8820.

Cascade Locks Chamber of Commerce and Visitors Bureau
(541) 374-8619
Hood River Visitors Bureau
(541) 386-2000.

PORTLAND

Portland Oregon Visitors Association
Three World Trade Center
26 W. Salmon
Portland, OR 97204
(800) 962-3700

Portland Parks and Recreation Department
Hoyt Arboretum
4000 Southwest Fairview Boulevard
Portland, OR 97221
(503) 823-3655

WASHINGTON

MOUNT ST. HELENS NATIONAL VOLCANIC MONUMENT

Gifford Pinchot National Forest
Mount St. Helens National Volcanic
Monument
42218 Northeast Yale Bridge Road
Amboy, WA 98601
(360) 750-3900

Mt. St. Helens National Volcanic Monument
Visitors Center
(360) 274-2100

Mt. St. Helens Climbing Hotline
(360) 750-3961

SEATTLE

Seattle-King County
Convention and Visitors Bureau
520 Pike Street, Suite 1300
Seattle, WA 98101
(206) 461-5800

Visitor Information Center–Downtown Seattle
Washington State Convention & Trade
Center
800 Convention Place, Galleria Level
(206) 461-5840

Underground Tour
610 First Avenue
Seattle, WA 98104
(206) 682-4646.

Seattle Parks Department
Recreation Information Office
5201 Greenlake Way
North Seattle, WA 98103
(206) 684-4075

Bainbridge Island Chamber of Commerce
590 Winslow Way E.
Bainbridge Island, WA 98110
(206) 842-3700

San Juan Island National Historical Park
P.O. Box 429
Friday Harbor, WA 98250
(206) 378-2240

OLYMPIC NATIONAL PARK

Olympic National Park
600 E. Park Ave.
Port Angeles, WA 98362
(206) 452-4501

Olympic National Forest
Quinault Ranger District
Quinault, CA 98575
(206) 288-2525

Lake Quinault Lodge
P.O. Box 7
Lake Quinault, WA 98575
(360) 288-2900.

MT. RAINIER NATIONAL PARK

Mt. Rainier National Park
Ashford, WA 98304
(360) 569-2211

Rainier Mountaineering, Inc.
Paradise, WA 98398
(360) 569-2227.

Mount Rainier Guest Services
55106 Kernahan Road East
Ashford, WA 98305
(360) 569-2275,

NORTH CASCADES NATIONAL PARK

North Cascades National Park
Sedro Woolley, WA 98284
(206) 856-5700

Lake Chelan National Recreation Area
P.O. Box 549
Chelan, WA 98816
(509) 682-2549

Mt. Baker-Snoqualmie National Forest
Mt. Baker Ranger District
Sedro Woolley, WA 98284
(206) 856-5700

Cascade Loop Association
P.O. Box 3245
Wenatchee, WA 98801
(509) 662-3888

Lake Chelan Boat Company
Box 186
Chelan, WA 98816
(509) 682-2224

Lake Chelan Tours
P.O. Box 1119
Chelan, WA 98816
(509) 682-8287.

Lake Chelan National Recreation Area shuttle bus
Reservations: (360) 856-5703, ext. 14.

North Cascades Institute
2105 State Route 20
Sedro Woolley, WA 98284
(360) 856-5700.

Ross Lake Resort
Rockport, WA 98283
(206) 386-4437

North Cascades Stehekin Lodge
P.O. Box 457
Chelan, WA 98816
(509) 682-4494

BRITISH COLUMBIA

VANCOUVER

Greater Vancouver Convention and Visitors Bureau
Suite 210, Waterfront Center
200 Burrard Street
Vancouver, B.C., Canada V6C 3L6
(604) 682-2222

Discover British Columbia
Information and Reservations Line
(800) 663-6000.

Granville Island Information Center
(604) 666-5784

Grouse Mountain Skyride
(604) 984-7234.

Rockwood Adventures Walking Tours
1330 Fulton Avenue
West Vancouver, BC
Canada, V7T 1N8
(604) 926-7705

VANCOUVER ISLAND

Tourism Association of Vancouver Island
45 Bastion Square, Suite 302
Victoria, B.C. V8W 1J1
(604) 382-3551

Goldstream Provincial Park
2930 Trans Canada Highway
R.R. 6, Victoria, B.C., V9B 5T9
(604) 391-2300

Coastal Connections (Walking & Eco-tours)
P.O. Box 8360
Victoria, B.C. V8W 3R9
(604) 480-9560

Pacific Rim National Park Reserve
Box 280
Ucluet, B.C. V0R 3A0
West Coast Trail Reservations:
(800) 663-6000

WHISTLER/GARIBALDI PROVINCIAL PARK

Garibaldi/Sunshine District
Box 220
Brackendale, B.C. V0N 1H0
(604) 898-3678

Whistler Activity and Information Center
(604) 932-2394

Index

ABOUT THE AUTHOR

Acclaimed nature writer John McKinney is the author of *A Walk Along Land's End*, a narrative of his 1,600-mile solo trek the length of the California coast. The longtime *Los Angeles Times* hiking columnist is the author of eight walking and nature guides. McKinney writes articles and commentaries about walking for national publications, promotes hiking and conservation on radio and TV, and serves as a consultant to the fast-growing walking products industry.